To M... Best wishes Julius Mercer 9/21

A NEW FIRE

By

JULIUS MERCER

As told to

Christopher W Graul

The author "Julius Mercer" reserves all rights, etc…

Cover Photo provided by, Ed Vetté Wilson Jones, Artist-In-Residence,
Tradesman, 1-773-761-2500
Board of Trustees, United Church of Rogers Park,
www.facebook.com/united-church-of-rogers-park

Contents

INTRODUCTION

In the Christian tradition, many congregations recite the "Apostle's Creed," part of which states as follows:

> "[Jesus] descended to the dead.
> On the third day he rose again."

The story you are about to read is a story of a man who was at the heights of attention and success: one of the nations' top 400-meter hurdles, Olympic trials participant, record-holder of his university.

But he fell, hard and far, into his own personal hell of drugs, promiscuity, and poverty. He went from paid international travels with attention and gifts, to literally begging for drug and meal money on the streets and sleeping in doorways.

And yet, as you will soon read, by utilizing the tools and resources offered him by counselors, family and friends, he is now able to say he "rose again."

I was introduced to Julius when he still was without a home of his own, when he was still early in recovery, and he gave me a copy of a draft manuscript of what he had written about his journey. He eventually asked me to put it into a narrative form. I found it a difficult, because Julius' life contains so many stories, each of which could be expanded into something much longer and larger.

Julius' life story is being offered because Julius wants his life lessons to maybe provide helpful guidelines and warning signals to others. If you have ever suffered depression, ever felt abandoned or doubted your value to others, ever saw yourself surrounded by darkness with no light showing a path out, ever been tempted to give up pursuing a successful life (however that is defined for you), then this book is for you.

If you know anyone who is going through emotional, legal or mental difficulties and you want desperately to help but don't know how to reach this person, then this book is for you.

If you just want to read a story about a man who lived a life of success, a man who lived total drug-induced failure, and a man who fought with all his strength to climb out of that black hole, then this book is for you.

Christopher W Graul, March 31, 2019

THE POWER OF FEAR

This is a story about overcoming: overcoming fear, defeats, loss, loneliness, abandonment -- overcoming a life I was willing to exchange for a hit of cocaine and a short night with any woman who happened to be nearby.

Beginning in 1995, I spent a total of 14 years of my life incarcerated. While in jail, awaiting the outcomes of alleged charges, each time I was sent to a mental ward, which provided me a more comfortable environment, and therapeutic treatment. When not locked up, I threw all of therapeutic advice and suggestions out of the window and did what I thought was best for myself, believing that my own self-will could promote me to be successful again. However, underestimating the importance of treatment plan's effect upon me, I instead spent my days hustling the streets and my nights in abandoned buildings, or bug-infested shelters until one day I woke up.

I looked around at what was left of my shattered life, and finally, in one of my few rational moments, asked myself: "What happened? How did I end up like this?"

I was raised in a normal household: one sister, three brothers, military father and loving mother. Although my father spent his life in the Army, willing to die for this country, he was also aware of and cautious of "being Black" in the wrong places. For example, we were once driving through the Tennessee Smoky Mountains when we were caught in a blinding snow storm. Most people would have --- and could have --- stopped at a motel for the night, had a nice meal in a nearby restaurant, and rested up for a new start the next morning.

We were not "most people." My father did not want to risk stopping and being rejected or, worse, perhaps attacked.
So we drove on; even when we stopped for gas, we did not dare use the bathrooms; my father told us to "just hold it in."

And so we did, as the car crawled along the sinewy mountain roads in the darkness until we were somewhere we felt safer.

When I was a child, everything was confusing and scary, even shocking, as I saw and heard racial bigotry in plain sight. While living in Virginia (I was nine), during the time of school desegregation tensions, I was so afraid during the race riots initiated by the KKK that I wanted to hide on the school bus. My father, a military man, and took time off from work and followed the Army National Guard to and from each county until the race tensions eased.

If you are Black in America, you will understand when I say "that's just how it was." After my father retired and we moved to Park Forest, Illinois in 1973, I discovered the joy of being the object of racial bullying.

I was 13 years old, and my two eldest brothers, Mike and Fred were direct targets of physical and verbal abuse from a secular fascist group of young radical white men who classified themselves as "Nazis."

They would spend their days terrorizing people of color or whites who were friends of (or even socialized with) people of color. There were many weekends and evenings when a close friend named Khallis and I were racially assaulted; we were the targets of hurled bottles, beers cans and sticks while on our way to play basketball at an after school program.

The same group that accosted us placed stickers all over the Park Forest community that read "white power" and featured a Nazi logo. In 1976, my eldest brother and his friends were attacked by more than 20 Nazis at the Park Forest Plaza. My brother Fred was hospitalized, which so angered my dad that he went looking for the Nazi gang with his Excalibur gun.

He didn't find them but my Dad spoke with the police chief, who assured him they would apprehend the thugs. Within one week, the police had captured the assailants, dispersed the group, and Park Forest has since become one of the greatest all-American cities in the nation.

This was, in large part, due to the city's cultural diversity. People of all ethnicities grew up together in relatively peaceful neighborhoods, with low crime rates and few racial confrontations.

The other kids at Rich East -- mostly the Whites but also occasionally some of the Black kids -- made fun of my complexion, my lips, my pacificity. What they could not deny was my athletic skills, which was where I set my mark and I learned to use my sense of humor to make my peace with schooling.

My grades were passable, not great. I was not a club joiner, and did not have many interests except doing the one thing I was best at: sports. I excelled at basketball, playing on a highly-rated team in 1978n (my junior year). Also on that team was two-time NBA champion Craig Hodges. Our coach was Steve Fisher, who gained fame coaching the famous Michigan Wolverines known as the "Fab Five."

(He recently retired from coaching at San Diego State University).

However, it was in track that I found my niche once I discovered the low hurdles, under coaches Lionel Poole and Johnny Meisner. I discovered my long legs made me a natural.

OPEN DOORS

I am going to mention several names in this chapter, and I have a very good reason for doing so: no one – no one – has ever reached a level of any success without a helping hand from others along the path. You hear about "self-made" men, who brag they "did it all themselves." This is not true. When they built their factory building, for example, who paid for the roads leading to their site? Who installed the electric wiring to that part of town? Who teaches their children in the local schools?

So every name I mention here is a person who helped me take one more step toward my destiny.I was driven by the values instilled in me by some of the country's best coaches: strong commitment, daily practices, and eliminating weaknesses. Keeping these phrases in my mind are what drove me to focus on improving my natural strengths to become a champion hurdler in world-class track and field competition.

But it was the work of others which led me to whatever success I achieved.

At Rich East High School, my eldest brother Fred referred me to the track coach, Larry Roland, who motivated me to join the track team. At that time, the Rich East team wasn't among the best in the State. Although new to hurdling, under Coach Meissner, (who had replaced Coach Roland), my skills improved at a tremendous rate. I remember learning that my hurdling buddy and teammate, Donald Hudspeth, signed a letter of intent to Butler Community College in Kansas. I had not even considered my track future after high school.

You might remember, earlier I mentioned that my failure to embrace the academic learning experiences or place a high priority on making good grades kept me from going to a major university after graduation. However, I saw that junior college was a viable option, so I followed Hudspeth and enrolled in Butler Community College.

Where again quality coaching, under Coach John Francis continued my hurdling improvement.

I attended Butler from 1979 to 1982. Besides the running, sprinting, and hurdling workouts (including practicing "coming out of the blocks" or starting, and minute technical work), the coaches also had me pull sleds: I would wear a vest made of carpeting, which was hooked to a 150-pound log, which I would drag up and down hills to gain upper and lower body strength. Coach Francis also had me doing 100 yard sprints repeatedly, along with sprinting quarter-mile turns into 40-50 mile per hour headwinds through the Kansas cornfields.

As a result of a disciplined and vigorous routine, I earned the honor of being a four-time (both high and low hurdles for two years) Junior College All-American Track and Field Athlete (110- and 400-Meter Hurdles). I was the first (and to date only) track athlete to accomplish this feat in Butler County College history.

I graduated Rich East High school with a 1.65 grade-point average (4.0 is the best; I was almost impossibly low). My English teacher at Butler evaluated me at 6th grade level for science, English, and math. But with a massive amount of help from tutors – who generously gave me their time and patience – I graduated from Butler with a 2.0 GPA, which enabled me to receive a full-ride scholarship to Kansas State University.

This was the result of efforts by Butler's Coach Francis, who recognized that I had no money and fought for me.

Meanwhile, news of my success in track and greater potential had spread across the region. I began receiving attention from a number of Division I Colleges and Universities such as the University of Nebraska, University of Oklahoma, the University of Kansas, University of Miami, Florida A&M and a host of others including many Division II Colleges. Ultimately, I chose Kansas State University, home of the Wildcats.

There were a number of reasons that I chose the Wildcats, however the determining factor was that I needed financial assistance and they offered a full-scholarship. My motivation was energized by a multitude of relationships with influential people in my life such as Coach Johnny Meisner, Peter Struck, Mr. Hynk, Larry Roland, Roger Bohnesteil, Dale Freundt, and Steve Fisher (current Coach of San Diego State University). All of these people had a tremendous impact on my life as a teenager while I was attending High School. These people taught me the values of hard work and being a good person. They guided me through high school while helping shape my conduct and taught me to be a good person.

This is where I learned what "character" meant. I believe many of the things they taught me helped to save my life. Mr. Lionel Poole, a high school Hall of Fame Track Coach, formerly of Bloom High School-Chicago Heights, Illinois.

He was responsible for negotiating a full track and field scholarship for me to attend Butler County Community College. He also gave me the vision to believe I could compete and succeed at the Division I level college sports and obtain an academic degree by successfully completing all of the necessary course requirements.

Education was the key, because it put me in a position to be mentored and developed by Coaches such as Hall of Fame track coach, Steve Miller and others like Ollie Isom, John Cappriotti, Gregg Kraft and John Francis, which catapulted me to a world class hurdler.

There were professors at Kansas State University such as Henry Camp and Marvin Kaiser who advised me to put quality time in at the library.

They encouraged me to research information on a particular subject matter related to my class assignments or to ask the Librarians for assistance.

One of my professors used a very unique and effective exercise with me: he told me to seek out a mentor who had overcome great obstacles in his or her life, then study and learn from that life. I chose Mr. Frederick Douglas, a man born into slavery during the 1800s. My reading showed me that illiteracy could not stop his internal drive to rise above racial injustices and educational inequality.

As a child, Frederick Douglas tricked his slave counterparts into teaching him how to read. He then escaped from being enslaved because he was able to read the directional signs, and headed north to Massachusetts where slavery was abolished.

Arriving there, Douglas eventually found comfort with new friends, married and began a family. He performed well in school and joined forces with other blacks and whites who had formed an Abolitionist Party.

This winning attitude of Mr. Frederick Douglas eventually manifested itself into the development of his natural intelligence, which had been suppressed when he was a slave. My mentor, Mr. Douglas, was an educated slave who soon escaped physical slavery in the deep southern territories of America to become an icon in the history of the African-American experience.

At the time, Kansas State was (and is) a track-and-field powerhouse; however, it did not reach its pinnacle until 3 years later.

During my 1982-83 junior year, I spent most of my time partying and chasing girls. I had no interest in studying and it showed. It also resulted in receiving a Letter of Dismissal. So my educational pursuits were seemingly at an end. However, the deans of the sociology college, Henry Camp and Marvin Kaiser, sat me down and explained the facts of life to me: I had a free scholarship, but if I leave school no one will care about me. I would be just another Black athlete who failed.

So, at their direction, I took four summer-school classes, with the mandate that I must receive no grade below a "B." Plus, I had to spend time with the tutor and studying in the library every Monday through Friday. I did everything they demanded, and received two "A" and two "B" grades, then received a letter from the university re-admitting me.

In 1983 (my senior year), the brilliant coach Steve Miller became the KSU track coach. Under Coach Miller, I learned how to perfect my form and cadence, and the value of hard work. We practiced timing the stretch between the hurdles, practiced counting the steps, practiced throwing the lead leg and pulling the trail leg properly over the unforgiving wooden barriers. Thousands of repetitions, early in the dew of morning, late in the setting sun --- and the results were almost immediate. Kansas State Coach Steve Miller enforced a rigorous training regimen that included:

1). No days off

2). 3-mile runs, twice per week

3). 6-mile runs once per week

4). Swimming pool workouts

5). Big Hill workouts

6). Weight-training

7). Watching our diet

I blossomed my senior year and set the university school record in the hurdles, and placed 3d at the NCAA Championship meet (I was the second American; more on that later). Thirteen years after graduation (in 1996), I was inducted into the prestigious Sports Hall of Honor at Kansas State University (now called the "Hall of Fame").

Following graduation (in July 1983), I went to Indianapolis for the National Track and Field Championships, where I competed in the 400-meter hurdles. Immediately prior to the gun, my former coach at Butler College, John Francis, implored me to not look back; keep eyes on the stagger runner in lane 6 (I was in lane 5).

Edwin Moses, perhaps the greatest hurdler in history, had won 75 consecutive finals to that point, and was looking for number 76, which would be a new record. Edwin was in Lane 4, next to me, but behind me at the start.

As I approached the first turn, I could see the lane 6 runner, and knew from the stagger distance that I was in good shape. However, I committed the cardinal sin: I turned to my left to check on where Edwin Moses was. As it happened, he was already on my shoulder. As you might expect, he blew away the field and won by 20 meters or so. Really, it was not much of a race.

Upon my graduation from Butler Community College in 1981, I attended my first recruiting trip to further my education. I visited with the University of Arkansas in Fayetteville, Arkansas, where I was greeted by one of the greatest triple-jumpers in track and field history, Mr. Mike Conley (today he is Mike Connelly, Sr.).

Mike Conley had come from Luther South high school in Chicago and later won a Gold Medal in the 1996 Olympic Games. Mike showed me a vision of what I could have as a result of furthering my education and excelling in athletics.

Mike led me on a two-day tour of the Razorbacks' beautiful multi-million dollar, state-of-the-art facility. Then he shared with me the importance of earning a degree. Mike was actually younger than I (a sophomore – 2nd year student, while I was entering as a junior).

The things I admired and most impressed me about Mike Conley was his sincere personality, humility, and his emphasis on education. He explained to me that as a teenager he had had no idea of life's possibilities, and had had no vision of himself as an all-around athlete in basketball and track and field. His emphasis and focus had always been on education: gaining knowledge, proper application, followed by graduation. Academic excellence was the key to all of his success in the athletic arena.

Mike had come from the inner-city communities, facing many of the obstacles I had of growing-up in a big complicated city, yet as an adult played a critical role with the City of Chicago's bid to host the 2016 Olympics in his position as Executive Director of World Sports Chicago. If he did it successfully, I thought, then so could I.

Because of my place in the NCAAs (second American in the low (400-meter) hurdles, I was selected to represent the USA in the World University Games in Edmonton, Canada that year.

In the 1983 Big Eight meet, I had run 13.79 in the high (110-meter) hurdles; in NCAAs that year, I finished the low hurdles in 49.7 (still the Kansas State record). These two times qualified me for the 1984 Olympic Trials.

However, prior to the USA Olympic Trials, I was invited to participate in a series of international meets, including the Japanese Olympic Trials in Tokyo.

This came about because of my performance at the USA National Track and Field meet the following year.

When I got to Japan, I was invited to the Mizuno factory; they were a sponsor of the trials. After showing me around the factory, they then gave me a bunch of gear, including a pair of shoes which, quite frankly, felt like cheap plastic. However, they then insisted that I wear these shoes during the Trials race and, in fact, mandated that I either wear their plastic shoes "or don't run." So I wore them, to my detriment.

I was given lane 4 (considered the prime lane), but came in fourth, in front of 65,000 spectators, all expecting the American in lane four to win and promote their shoes. Mizuno, of course, was unhappy with my finish, and I was unhappy with their crappy shoes.

Three weeks later, at the end of July 1984, was the USA Olympic Trials in Los Angeles. Steve Miller, my coach at Kansas State, was quoted in the university yearbook as follows:

"Their intensity is much greater simply because of the idea of the Olympic Games— you see people in a different setting; one that you've never seen before,"

Miller said. Because of the competitiveness, Miller believes that K-State will have its share of athletes in the Games.

*"There are three to four people who have a shot at making it — Doug Lytle,Kelly Wenlock, Veryl Switzer and **Julius Mercer**. After those four, it will be a pretty tight race" Miller said. One of the people Miller feels strongly about is Mercer. Two years ago, Mercer was unknown in the Big Eight Conference. But, after last season's showing in the intermediate hurdles, winning the Big Eight outdoor and finishing high in the NCAA Indoor and Outdoor champion-ships, Mercer has steadily become a known athlete.*

"Julius is going to have to run his lifetime best at the right time," Miller said of Mercer's chances in the trials.[1]

[1] --- *1983 Kansas State University, "Royal Purple Yearbook," page 246.*

During training, for the Olympic Trials, I was working as a graduate assistant to Coach Miller at KSU; one day, during training, I noticed a pain in my left knee. One of my training procedures was to set up 6 hurdles, clear them, and then have a long sprint to the finish. I would then reverse it: sprinting the track, then finishing with 6 hurdles. During one of these exercises, I came down on my left leg and felt something that was not right. I decided not the tell anyone, and instead went to a doctor to have it looked at. The doctor told me I needed it "scoped," (arthroscopy) and recommended I not run on it. But with the Olympics so close, I ignored his advice and continued to train, keeping the injury secret.

At the trials, my qualifying time had me ranked sixth overall and second in my heat in the low hurdles. When I cleared the final hurdle, I had about ten meters on the rest of the field, and, because my final sprint had always been my strength, I was apparently going to be the easy winner.

But fate had another idea. As I began the final sprint, I felt my knee explode with pain and all my power left me. I could not thrust my leg forward. The other runners caught me, leaving me just shaking my head in frustration.

I had not only failed to make the Olympic team; I had not even gotten out of the preliminaries.

"HELP ME, SON!"
MARRIAGE LIFE AND MY FATHER

In 1985, while I was working as an assistant track coach at Butler College, I met a woman whom I thought was the perfect one for me:

I had spent the previous two years getting my life together: coaching, maturing, thinking of my future. One of my college roommates, Darrel Anderson (now the women's track coach at TCU) inspired me to leave the partying behind and grow up. So, socially, in 1985, I was socially adrift. I had been a track star, travelling to exotic (for me) countries, getting attention, being promoted, shaking hands, having ribbons placed around my neck. But I had no *anchor*, no special person who I knew would be there for me to listen, to hold, to *know who I was.*

Then I met Theresa Walker, in the spring of 1985, and she offered me quiet time, a respite from the hectic travel and attention, and wanted me for who I actually was; I jumped and felt I had found sanctuary. We married three months later, in Kansas City. However, I had received an offer to run for the South Bay Track Club in Los Angeles, and a guarantee of a job. I was also allowed to bring with me two of my Butler athletes. Of course, who wouldn't want to go to LA: palm trees, sun, beaches!

Theresa refused to go with me to LA unless we were married, so we married. Then unexpectedly, the big BOOM! My marriage was ending, under the terms of "irreconcilable differences." It all ended after a seven-year span. Six of these years were the greatest years of our lives. We enjoyed many wonderful, joyous and adventurous times. We had FUN! We were both exercise, health and fitness nuts, and we had lots of fun together. The seventh year brought a whirlwind of decisions, issues and changes.

My wife was pregnant with our first child. I was extremely happy but found myself unable to deal with the changes that go along with pregnancy (like adjusting to a major reduction in physical intimacy and emotional affection). I felt my grasp on what and who had been my emotional support system was loosening, and I did not handle it well. Perhaps this was an indicator of some immaturity on my part, but regardless, our relationship was changing. A relationship that was once built on mutual compromises, mutual trust, and mutual respect had degraded to uncompromising differences and feelings of rejection on both sides.

The Lamaze pregnancy training classes were helpful, but they could not prepare me for that moment when our daughter was born and they said she wasn't breathing. I panicked, and screamed, "Oh no!" They said that her esophagus and nostrils were closed with defecation.

The doctors quickly attempted to clear the blockage by using a syringe as a siphon technique. I yelled her name, "Jessica!"

My little baby daughter opened her eyes, stared at me and then began to cry. I cried too, realizing that a miracle had been born. I cried so much that I could barely see. I looked forward to showing her off to everyone: my family, everyone I knew, and the entire community of Park Forest.

We divorced when our child was two months old, but I held tight to the possibility of reconciliation; unfortunately, that hope was destroyed when I learned that my former wife re-married within three months of the divorce. I was caught up in the "how's" and "whys:" we had had what I thought was a wonderful life together, and now, for reasons I suspected were connected to the intrusion of my mother-in-law, I was being treated like an outcast.

Just five months before, when my child was born, I was elated. I went from being the happiest man on earth to being utterly crushed.

During the course of my divorce, I voluntarily surrendered my paternal rights to my ex-wife and her new husband due to my illness of depression. It was one of the most painful decisions I had ever made in my entire life; however, I thank God that I had the wherewithal to not be so self-centered, but be willing to do what was in the best interest of my child. My Dad, who became my rock in this storm, advised me to just focus on getting myself together and that someday my biological daughter would search for me, and guess what, years later she did!

At the time, though, I had to learn to stay focused daily, because I could feel stress slowly starting to take over parts of my life. Spiritual maintenance, especially thankful prayer had become a daily routine for me, and I was slowly being pulled away from this foundation.

In retrospect, there were many factors that led to my divorce.

Our inability to compromise, my inability to cope with the hormone changes that my ex-wife went through, and my own psychological and emotional changes, along with some self-centeredness on both our parts destroyed what was once a relatively beautiful relationship. My wife and I considered health and intelligence high priorities, and this seemed to lead us through a short successful relationship, but it was ultimately unable to sustain our relationship through the big important changes of life. Obviously, we didn't have the fortitude and passion to overcome the difficulties of life together, or the maturity that comes with adult development.

One month after my divorce, my dad – who had been always reserved and emotionally removed -- and I began to finally nurture the most meaningful bond I could have hoped for. That bond was built on honesty. Dad recognized that I was at the end of my rope. He talked to me with honesty and transparency, sharing examples from his past.

He admitted to me that he felt that he had not always been the best father or husband, but his wife – my mother – always stayed by his side, supporting and forgiving him each time.

His forthrightness helped me over my stumbling blocks and solidified a stronger bond of positive affection, love and openness between us. This allowed me to express my anger and share my problems positively and without negative rebellion. His willingness to listen, and to become a consoling counselor, provided comfort and let me know that my prior rebelliousness toward him could be abandoned. It was the search for comfort, for love, for hope, which had caused so much of my confrontational attitudes, and had caused the deep rupture in our relationship. Now, finally, I knew for the first time that my father actually and deeply loved me. I knew I would rebel no longer.

Then, on May 26, 1996, my dad had a massive heart attack. It had been sudden, with no prior warning.

Neither the paramedics (led by a high school friend of mine, Paul Hodges), nor my panicked life-saving attempts could put the breath of life back into my dad. I watched helplessly as the cardiac monitor flat-lined. My mom yelled, "Is everything alright Julius?" Caught up in a whirlwind of anger, disbelief, shock, and hopelessness, I couldn't muster enough courage to give a response. My father died in my arms. We buried him June 1. His very last words echoed endlessly through my mind. "Help me son." He was only 63 years old.

I immediately regressed and entered into the world of severe depression. The accumulation of stress from my divorce, the death of my father, and bad memories overwhelmed me and dropped me into a deep state of depression. I kept photographs of my wife and baby daughter throughout my apartment, and each time I saw one of the photos I would start to break down.

I learned later that sadness and depression are two different things: Sadness comes and goes with a particular situation or circumstance, but my Depression started out as sadness, but soon destroyed my emotional stability, taking hold of all rational thought and eroding it, and eroding it further, until I could no longer even muster the strength to care. I cried a lot and, soon, couldn't sleep unless I had a drink. I was constantly thinking about my problems and feeling sorry for myself 24-hours a day.

I suffered in silence; disguising the suffering as best I could I trudged through gray day after gray day. I was exhausted, had a loss of appetite, and lost interest in almost everything. My self-esteem was at an all-time low and I actually couldn't have cared less. Nothing in my life had value to me: not my friends, my family, my former dreams, money, health. All gone from my mind.

Bad memories, conscious and sub-conscious, kept me awake during the night. I began making very poor choices, turning like a storm-tossed boat in a night-time whirlpool to promiscuity, going from one woman to another with no care or thought of the possible effects on them or on me. The habit of sexual one-night stands charges its toll; in my case, it eventually led me to a place where cocaine was commonplace.

I underestimated the deadly powerful combination of untreated depression, unresolved issues, hurtful memories, and man-made synthetic drugs. This dangerous conflagration triggered a neuron-chemical imbalance called psychosis. I'm blessed and cursed to be able to recall the many delusions and hallucinations I had so that I can share it with you in this book.

I was hearing voices and sounds that were not verbalized. I was running from emergency vehicles; paranoia had me believing they were all a part of an assassination team.

The most painful recollection that sometimes still brings tears to my eyes was the belief that my family was part of the plot to kill me and that I would have to take either my own life or theirs before they all killed me.

I had become spiritually bankrupt.

MISSING VALUES, MISSING IDENTITY, MISSING LIFE

What are the most important things in life? Money? Love? Partying? Courage? Happiness? Is it Passion, freedom, respect, health, family?

None of these were of any value to me. When I thought on them (which was rarely), it was as if seeing a bad television show: I saw these parts of a full life, and had no interest in them. Values guide our decisions and life choices and I had no values.

It all began with my divorce, which devastated me, and very soon after that I had to endure the untimely death of my father. He actually died in my arms. Almost immediately I became angry at the world, God, the police, and the paramedics. This anger caused me to suffer a severe depression. I just did not care anymore. My attitude about these events changed my outlook on life.

Before my depression, my values kept me on track and kept me from doing drugs or hanging out with those who violated the law; but the depression weakened my values and began leading me down a path of self-destruction. Soon, I began to spiral downhill at breakneck speed. Not only did I start hanging out with people who used and sold drugs, I began to get sucked into the drug culture with them. In early 1993, I met up with a woman whom I had known slightly in the past. We started to hang out together; I was unaware that she was a crack cocaine user until one night I was at her place – along with a second woman friend – and they suggested that I try crack with them. To this point, I had had no interest in anything stronger than occasional weed (in high school and college). But I had been drinking this particular night (being separated from my wife and child had exposed my mental and psychological vulnerability toward depression) and they told me that smoking a little crack would alleviate the effects of the alcohol.

The drinking had lowered my inhibitions and, so, I agreed, thus beginning a nightmare (seeking the combination of crack and sex) that would haunt me for the better part of 25 years, a quarter-century of my life sucked away.

A couple weeks after my first encounter with cocaine, this same woman asked me to buy some crack for her, but I had no money. She angrily insisted I find money however I needed to find it, and buy her the crack she so desperately needed. Because my mind was not right, I agreed.

I went to a nearby apartment complex, broke into an apartment, and stole a VCR (for those of you who have no idea what a 'VCR" is: it was an analog "video recorder" that was the precursor of DVDs). I was caught and spent my first night in jail. So here I was, two months before me father passed; I was struggling with my divorce and its depression, but now I had two huge problems: deep depression compounded by a drug addiction.

My life spiraled downward quickly. I lost my jobs, my friends, my contacts with my family. I was living on the streets and in flop-houses and missions. My clothing (once a source of pride with me), always so clean and nice, deteriorated along with my life and were now dirty, uncared-for, ill-fitting. I guess they were a prefect outside image of what I had become on the inside.

At times, I asked myself: How could this have happened to me? I had been an accomplished and caring social worker and substitute teacher. How could such a strong, positive, high energy person like me have risen to such heights, only to fall so far down into the valley? Many times some of my former students saw me on the streets with my dirty clothes on; depressed, hungry, with uncombed hair and sleep in my eyes.

One particularly startling event occurred during this time: I had once counseled two high school students who had been going through bad times, doubting themselves, unmotivated.

I had spent a lot of time with them, counseling them, sitting with them, and trying to help them believe in themselves. Then, one night, I found myself – as usual – sitting in a jail cell. I looked around at my "cellies" in with me and there, across from my bed, were these two young men. What must they have thought, as I, who once had tried to steer them in the right direction, was now down in the same low life as they, just a few short years later. In another jail a short time later (I seemed to have spent time in all of the nearby iron-bar hotels), I shared a tier with four of my former mental health clients. How could I ever again be an example, or offer help or encouragement, when I was swimming in the same swirling waters? In the movie "The Pursuit of Happiness" Will Smith played Chris Gardner, a real life individual who was down on his luck: living in poverty, wearing dirty smelly clothes, living in shambles, with a small son to raise, he never backed down from life. He continued to believe in the future.

One day, he took saw an ad for an open job, and took a chance and applied. Of course, he had no money to buy new clothes, but nevertheless he showed up to the job interview. Seated before him was a panel of some very powerful corporate executives at a brokerage firm. Gardner (Will Smith) appeared with paint in his hair, wearing grubby clothes and breath that could knock down a dinosaur. He got the job, despite his dishevelment and odor, because of his beliefs and values. His values were the threads of beliefs sown deeply in his heart and soul which shaped and molded his character. His values were family, integrity, courage, determination, perseverance, communication skills, self-control, and most importantly; when he was hurt and angry he did not use alcohol, drugs or fall into depression. He simply BELIEVED! When I watched that movie, I cried like a baby.

Afterwards, I called my mother and said through tears, "That's me!" She asked, "Why are you crying," and I replied, "I don't know why, mother, but I can feel his challenges."

I do not know everything; maybe I do not know much. But I have learned that to achieve goals, we all must BELIEVE that we can do it!

NEW POSSIBILITIES

Have you ever felt like you were not talented enough, smart enough, good looking enough or popular enough? I have felt all of these things. I felt I was a failure at life, with no door to success or happiness. One night, when I was living in LA, I remember driving home and I saw one of the omni-present helicopters overhead. I thought – inexplicably and irrationally, I now know – that the helicopter was searching for me. I was not rational enough to know who it was or why they were looking for me, but there it was.

I stopped my car, jumped out, and ran into a nearby backyard to hide. I didn't even know where I was, I only knew terror which was making my heart beat through my chest and my perspiration burn through my clothes. I eventually made it back to my house, running between yards. Any rational thought of a life with any peace was gone from my mind.

How to get from paranoia, constant drug use, burglarizing, serial jail visits, loss of family support, loss of home ... to a life of pride, loving relationships, clear-eyed mornings of hope and optimism?

The answer to overcoming these negative feelings and living victoriously is continuing, but it began with a true desire to have a better life. I had seen the possibilities and somewhere, buried beneath the detritus, was an awareness of what could be.

I knew I could not be intimidated by those who would tell me that I can't achieve greatness, because the answers are not in those naysayers; they were in me, and they are within each of us.

I am not a Sunday-morning preacher who has not been through the hard days and mindless nights of doubt and blackness. I have waded the rushing streams and gotten to the other side.

It was not books which have instructed me on change; it is coming to realize that, all this time, I had the power to overcome, to WIN, within me! It might have been deeply buried, but I had made the decision to dig it up and give it the light of day.

We each have this same power within us. The power is believing that you can do it. If we don't accept that we are a problem, then we can see that the doubters, those who are so quick to point to us with their negativity, are the ones with a problem is - they have to cut us down in order to feel good about themselves.

I am going to speak directly here to any person reading this who feels abandoned by hope: Unleash your power by making decisions you have been putting off. You won't believe the energy and excitement this will create for your life. That's why I am here today, because I followed my ideas and beliefs to help others achieve success in their lives. I have a passion and I BELIEVE! Just don't quit!

Here are some of the negative beliefs many of us hear while growing up. "You're stupid; you are not smart enough to go to college (I was told that); you will never be rich; you can't do anything right; you are not good enough so why should you even try; people aren't interested in what you have to say; boys don't cry; nobody cares what you have to say." Sound familiar?

I have learned that if we always do our best, the outcome will be positive. Doing our best is the spirit of constructive passion. When we dive headfirst to beat a baseball throw aimed to get us out at home plate, not worrying about getting hurt, that's passion.

It is passion that drives an inventor to keep going until her dreams become a reality. Great ideas help and improve our life conditions.

To stop dwelling on those negative statements, I had to figure out how they ingrained themselves in me, and kept me from learning more about myself and the great things I am capable of achieving.

For instance, how do I stop the fear of feeling stupid if I ask a question in school? My grades in high school were low because of this fear. I was the type of youngster who always wanted to learn new things. When I believed I could do things right, I saw that I got better at doing them; and each time persevered, I improved. Once I created a new belief, I found I needed to plant it firmly in my mind by repeating it over and over again every time a negative thought threatened to intrude. Psychologists say that 90% of our behavior is habit, and I had lived through good habits and bad, and I prefer the good! I examined my behavior and daily actions, and realized I was living out of habit.

When to rise each day, shower in the morning or evening, how much milk I put in my cereal, which candy bars I buy --- these are all habitual. I began to study the stories of great successes: how did someone, born the same as I (naked and crying) end up a successful leader, or a great inspiring teacher, or an inventor of something that changes the world (think of Edison and the light bulb, or Apple and the smartphone), or a billionaire? These great individuals became great, I observed, because they found something for which they were willing to go all out. These great people erased fear and found their passion and power. They didn't live in habit, but in exploration of possibilities. I had to find my passion, find fuel for my heart and soul. I knew that God had put into me everything I needed to be successful.

CAUGHT UP WITH THE "WHY'S"

What happened? This is probably the most common question posed to people who reach high levels of success or celebrity status early in life and then watch it all collapse.

For me, it started when I began to focus on the negative things like why and how I was doing wrong. Why me, why do these things happen to me when I have tried to treated others respectfully and fairly? I became really frustrated: "why is the world this way when it could be better?"

I now know that whatever we focus on the most is often what we will end up becoming. If we focus and visualize ourselves as failures, we will become failures. If we visualize our positive goals, we can reach those goals.

I chose to focus on the negatives; the bad treatment and unfairness, and as a result, I became a negative person.

Little did I know, I was giving up on my future hopes and dreams. Anger directed inward equals depression. While a person can be born with a chemical imbalance or depression, meaning it's endogenous, most depression is caused by over-thinking. What we perceive or feel is a negative emotion that makes us angry is actually a warning sign that something needs our attention. When we become familiar with this sign, then the emotion will become our friend. With the exception of only a couple of close friends (Rich and Sandy Reynoso), I lied to everyone I had cared about, telling them that I was all right, everything was honky-dory. But the truth was that my life had become an empty fraud. For the very first time, I now truly understand how real post-traumatic, post-partum stress and depression is, along with other facets of pre-disposed mental illness or an illness that is the result of unresolved bitter anger and explosive negative thoughts and how they can impact our lives (and, by extension, the rest of society).

The Honorable Congressman Bobby Rush of Chicago speaks with great concern about this sickness. Throughout the years, there have been news reports of women driving their vehicles into deep waters or people who have thrown children out of windows, reports of terrible child abuse, death, and how this deadly cycle has taken the lives of many innocent people who still had lives full of potential.

While employed in the field of social services, my training certification classes taught me the details and complexities of severe mental illness; however, I had no idea that real life practical experience would soon be my best teacher.

I had no clue of the actual effects of untreated mental illness. I understand why there needs to be a finding available of "not guilty by reason of insanity." Untreated depression will become only more severe.

One night, during my horror, my mind told me to get a knife and kill myself or my family.

Only the grace of God's divine intervention stopped me and told me to put the knife back. I firmly believe this was not an illusion, but a true miracle. My mother and sister were unaware how close we all came to a tragic event, but a few hours later, my sister and mother took me to the hospital for treatment.

Thank God for their unconditional love and the love of family that would stand beside me and see me through all my nightmares.

I began to recall how my dad and mom were raising us as children, teaching us to respect all adults, regardless of their skin color or ethnic origin.

It was as if my mind was stuck on negative memories and set on instant replay. I couldn't shake the thoughts of how hatred wouldn't allow us, a Black family, to lodge at hotels/motels overnight because of the color of our skin. (an odd irony: go to any resort or public beach in the world and you will see white people trying to become darker!

THEY'RE JUST LIKE I AM

I tend to push harder when things are going well. However, when things weren't going so well, I became hard on myself (have you had this feeling before?). I had to work on improving my attitude; finding the right balance and discovering the positive lessons that come out of bad situations.

Rather than live in accordance with the good values taught by my mom and dad, the values that once held me to a good and healthy set of high standards, I took another route, abandoning the sources of strength. I was living a life of pain and pleasure. As a result, promiscuity got the best of me. As I mentioned earlier, I began to look for quick gratification in terms of affection through prostitution, which ultimately led me down a dark path of drugs, despair and destruction of self-esteem. I had to take several AIDS tests (which fortunately proved to be negative). Somehow, I did not contract any STD's.

As bad as it was, I also learned a lot about people with more severe drug habits then I had. We all suffered from the very same things, such as depression, a relationship gone sour, death of a close loved one, physical or mental abuse, or rejection and bad memories of unresolved issues. In the midst of my promiscuity, I had a child out of wedlock. I initially rejected my new daughter, because her mother told me it the father might be me, and just as likely could be another man. Her family and mine believed the little girl looked just like me. She was born when I was in prison; when I got released almost two years later and saw this beautiful little girl, I saw myself reflected in her face. My drug habit had now really spiraled out of control, and consequently, I was only in her life for five months before being locked up again for burglary, related to my addiction. Knowing that I was not a good father also added to my imbalance and lowered my self-esteem.

At times I really felt a sense of total helplessness, and all of these experiences were being left untreated. I did not see my daughter Symiria again until she was almost five years old.

Destruction was seemingly inevitable and imminent.

Most people who have a heroin or cocaine habit do not continue to smoke (blow) or shoot-it-up just because they continue to enjoy the high; it's that the withdrawal pains are so severe. This is an actual, physical, dependence. A fellow inmate at the Cook County jail explained to me that when he decided to quit, he went cold-turkey; and for the next two days he locked himself in his bedroom and was literally crawling on his hands and knees. He instructed his wife not to open the door, come in or give in to his screams or commands to go and find him some heroin.

Heroin affects the entire nervous system and once the system is exposed to a certain level or continuous amount, the brain's pleasure center, which is stimulated by the nervous system, develops a massive craving that the average person cannot fathom or imagine. The withdrawal process totally obliterates the addict physically, virtually shutting down all movement.

Drinking more heavily and using hard drugs gave me a temporary sedation of feeling good, and as each day passed, I wanted relief, to feel that false sensation of good. It was fuel to destroy my dreams. I allowed Pride to lull me into a false sense of strength. I began to believe that I was too smart to allow the drugs and depression to do me in like other people, but I was wrong. I was an empty vessel. Emptiness, loneliness, guilt and resentment were my best friends. The innate intestinal fortitude that once helped catapult me to becoming a world-class hurdler was now a mass inside my body and brain, filled with a loss of hope.

I was just like they were and they were just like I was. Ninety percent of those incarcerated in the jails and prisons have commonalities related to untreated, unresolved family and relationship issues that went horribly wrong.

One of my cell-mates (whom I will call Tony), was a 500 lb. male who lived with an alcoholic mother. On a daily basis, Tony stayed filthy-drunk and was physically and verbally abusive. Tony explained how he watched helplessly as one of his brothers had died without warning and how he had been unable to ride in the ambulance, because he was too drunk and too busy arguing with others who were just as drunk. Tony was charged with domestic violence. He felt that these charges were false and were the result of having to deal with his mother during her alcoholic phases. At the time of Tony's arrest, his mom was "sleeping it off." I then began to share my story with him, hoping it might empower him with the life – changing impact of knowing that "*someone else was just like me*."

I believe that a true and intimate relationship with God matters most and is the beginning of recovery and victory, but as much as Tony needed God, he also needed helpful strategies to cope. After a night of sharing, Tony smiled, wiped his eyes, and we gave each other a high-five. Even in the midst of my own struggles to get back in the race of life, I never gave up. I would somehow get back up. I kept trying again and again, even though it wasn't easy.

Tony agreed to seek therapy. Therapy can be administered by different types of supportive services such as teachers, counselors, and/or preachers. Personally, I recommend finding a person with refined skills in this field of study. I enjoy telling my story to others because I have seen how it can help others with similar issues. It can help people similarly afflicted to open up, making them feel comfortable, and most importantly, they can begin to really understand their experiences and feelings.

Holding everything in and not sharing my feelings gave me a false sense of reality. I began stealing from and manipulating my family and friends. Abandoned buildings and abandoned cars were a great relief for my body which was weakened by the drugs and lack of nutrition. I began to look just like them, thinking I was so different. I now realize this unfortunate part of my journey would help me to see the world in a whole new way. They were just like me, someone who had tasted a normal life of experiences, struggles and challenges, but made some really poor decisions. However, with the memories of my parents' values and my coaches' motivational statements, my survival instincts kicked in and brought me back.

EDUCATION IS THE KEY

Often teenagers don't place a high priority on the value of education or place intelligence high on their list of values.

During the successful years of my track and field career, I rubbed elbows with some of the greatest athletes in the world. In one year alone, 1984, I met, became friends with, and competed on the same national platform with some great Olympians such as Edwin Moses (two-time Olympic hurdles champion) and Greg Foster (silver medalist in the hurdles) of UCLA, Greg was also one of my hometown comrades from Maywood, Illinois.

But the story I want to tell you is about and amazing 5ft. - 3in. young-lady, originally from Morocco and later Iowa State University. Her name is Nawal el Moutawakil. Nawal had developed a fascination with the 400 – meter hurdles (which is what I ran, but remember, I am 6' 4", and Nawal is only a little over five feet tall. The hurdles are 36 inches high).

However, being a woman in a conservative Muslim country, Nawal had to train in very restrictive clothing which covered her almost completely. Even at that, she suffered taunting and abuse from the men of Morocco, who did not countenance a woman running on their tracks in a sport no Moroccan woman had ever undertaken. She qualified for the first–ever woman's 400-meters at the 1984 Olympics, held in Los Angeles (it was also the first time women were allowed to compete in the marathon). When she shocked the track world by winning the first women's gold medal ever awarded in the event, she became also the first Moroccan athlete – man or woman - to ever win a gold medal in ANY Olympic event. No woman from a Muslim country had ever won an Olympic gold medal in any sport.

Nawal of course obtained a college degree at Iowa State. She took advantage of both her athletic opportunities and education;

after retiring from competition, Nawal was appointed to the IAAF ("International Association of Athletics Federations," which governs international competitions in track) board and, in, after becoming a member of the IOC (International Olympic Committee) in 1998, was appointed to its Executive Board in 2008. She served as Chairperson of the IOC Coordination Commission for the 2016 Olympics in Rio de Janeiro and actually became a part of the government of Morocco, first as minister of youth and sports and later (1997 – 1998) as the secretary of state for the department.

This woman has lived an amazing story, which is inspiring not just because she overcame cultural and historical prejudices to compete and succeed, but because she used her platform to advocate for and help install meaningful, real changes in her country. Women now compete regularly in all Olympic sports and many countries have developed excellent training facilities open to women that match that of those offered to men.

And Ms. Nawal el Moutawakil has played a huge role in this transformation, with repercussions all over the world.

I take two lessons from this story: The first is that the obstacles we face are NEVER insurmountable. If this woman can persevere and succeed in overcoming the disdain and obstacles erected by an entire regional history, then I know, if I set my mind on the goals and work tirelessly toward them, I can also succeed. Maybe not to her level, but certainly succeed at what life offers me.

The second lesson is the importance of grabbing onto the opportunities offered. Nawal had the opportunity to go to college, and she went, where she then saw the opportunity to compete in the hurdles, and she did it.

She did not quit, did not allow negative "I can't do this" thinking to limit her possibilities. A college education opened doors to success.

These people represented some of the greatest moments in the history of the Olympics, particularly over the past few decades.

My life was going pretty well and was (and is) an example of how important education is. Eventually in life, education will aid in the development of a person's ability to make intelligent decisions, for the most part. Education put me in this world-class atmosphere. During these years, I didn't live too high and I didn't live too low, but I was happy. While attending Butler County Community College in Kansas, I had some trouble in academics. My weak areas were basic Math, Algebra, and English. I truthfully did not know how to write a complete sentence or put into written words the proper paragraphs needed to correctly articulate my thoughts and complete a written essay. I was on the verge of losing my athletic scholarship due to poor grades (although, in all honesty, also because I tried to out-slick the track coach by risking injury playing in a basketball tournament in the local City Leagues).

The obvious fact is that many athletes become spoiled; we are given "passes" in many courses simply because we are athletes. In fact, however, this "help" that teachers and professors give us so freely often ends up being a true detriment to our lives. We do not learn consequences; we never have to confront the requirements of living in a structured society.

As a result, one of the biggest struggles talented athletes experience, is that doubt in the back of their minds that they may not have the aptitude to grasp the basic fundamentals of academic studies.

During my years at Kansas State University, I had the pleasure of meeting a variety of very good people who became my friends. I really did have a misconception about the people of Kansas.

My early thoughts were formed by my ignorance and perhaps experience with other white and black southerners.

I thought they were just hillbillies, rednecks and slow, country black folks. I found that the vast majority of these people were kind-hearted, caring, and down to earth people who enjoyed life, laughter, agriculture and sports. The State of Kansas and its people have always been good to me. They represent some of the finest citizens in America.

Without the proper education, both yesterday and today, I would likely be making misinformed decisions about people for the rest of my life. Education is the key.

PEOPLE ARE THE KEY

Through the support and counseling of great people at Butler Community College, I began to understand that wonderful physical attributes can only get you so far in life. We are all guaranteed to get older and will eventually reach some physical limitations; however, our brains have a greater capacity to continue to receive, study, and calculate information, reason logically, and determine solutions and strategies.

We all can reach out and grab the opportunity to continue to explore, create and achieve. The faculty at Butler assigned me to special classes that helped me overcome my deficiencies. When Coach Francis discovered that I was playing basketball, he chewed me out and threatened to take away my scholarship. I believe his biggest disappointment was that I had been dishonest with him. However, he had a special love for and sincere dedication to his athletes.

Once he read me the riot act, it became real to me. I understood I had a decision to make. I thought to myself, "not my scholarship! I don't want to go back home." I begged, "Coach, please give me another chance!" Coach did not give me a favorable response immediately. Something inside of me said, "Go talk to another Coach." I went and talked to Coach Kohls. He had an uncanny ability to deal with student relations in a very bold, insightful, and compassionate manner, unlike what I had experienced with any other person who was born and bred in Kansas. He commanded, demanded and expected only one thing, and that was respect. He kept it real, and he shot straight from the hip. After explaining my problem, he had a discussion with Coach Francis and it apparently helped to calm my track coach down quite a bit. A few days later, Coach Francis apologized for snapping at me and then calmly explained why it was so dangerous and a huge risk for me to be playing basketball.

(wow, he obviously saw something special in me, that I did not know at that time).

He said "I want you to enjoy this college experience and have fun. I know that you like basketball, but be very careful with your decisions, because if you get hurt, no one will continue paying for your education and I want you to graduate without having to pay out of your pocket."

(I later learned that Coach Kohls and Coach Francis had grown up together. As of 2009, Mr. Kohls is head of student recruitment at Butler Community College. If you are considering a college to attend or encouraging your kid to attend, give Mr. Kohls a call for a great opportunity to attend a fine institution of higher learning, great sports and an overall great college experience.)

I am forever grateful to Butler Community College and its staff and faculty. Remember where I spoke earlier of the effect Mike Conley had on me when I visited University of Arkansas?

Mike demonstrated, with his life, the lesson he consistently repeated and which I still hold dear: "Education is the Key". I learned to talk, talk, and talk with coaches, teachers and counselors. I found ways to go about putting myself in a position to achieve my true, whole potential.

Because of people like Mike Conley, my inspiration, focus and drive were highly stimulated to set higher personal standards to achieve by giving my best to both sports AND education.

I believe with all my heart that everyone in the world has some type of raw talent or potential that can be nurtured and brought out with the help and guidance of the right influences. It takes a combination of people who care to find out what you can offer to society, your family and yourself. I was able, with the help and guidance of so many people, to excel athletically and academically. Seeing the vision, establishing a plan and setting goals were paramount on the journey.

I had a goal to shoot for in track and field; the Olympics. I wanted to become an honored member of the 1984 United States Olympic Team.

Education teaches us how to observe things and research information. I learned to observe my competition and study the best athletes and their techniques. The target of this "research" were those who had already made a name for themselves, and were considered by their colleagues, sports-writers and coaches to be the best in the field. My coaches would say, "Watch how they stretch and warm-up;" I noticed the top track and field athletes would separate themselves from everyone else to gain better focus and concentration. My target was the greatest 400-meter hurdler in the world: the great Mr. Edwin Moses. Edwin Moses, a graduate of Morehouse College, was in a sense my idol. Mr. Moses was an undefeated Olympic Champion in 1976, and he recited the Olympic oath on behalf of the 1984 Olympic team.

Two months prior to the 1984 Olympic Games I experienced what was perhaps the greatest moment in the pursuit of my goal. Even today the memory is as vivid as photographic recall; almost tactile memories of a split-second during competitions in Indianapolis, Indiana at the United States Track and Field Championships.

This meet attracted the largest number of media in the history of U.S. Track and Field, particularly for the 400 meter hurdles. Edwin Moses had entered the event with, I believe, 110 straight victories -- and one more win would set a new record for consecutive wins. This was the backdrop to one of the most dramatic events of my life. Nine men had qualified for the final showdown and wow, I had surprised even myself by not only qualifying for the big showdown, but finishing with a qualifying time only a second behind Edwin Moses. He was in Lane 4 and I was in 5. The race was being televised on a national network by ABC's Wide-World of Sports (the ESPN of my era).

These conditions alone gave me butterflies. Here I was on the national stage with some of the world's best athletes and I can't believe all of this is happening so fast.

As each runner lined up behind the starting blocks, the television coordinator instructed us to relax due to a television time-out (a major golf tournament was also in progress and being televised). During the time-out, I asked Edwin Moses to sign an autograph of a picture for me and I said, "Please sign it to Richard Reynoso, he's a dear family friend of mine."

Edwin smiled while glancing at me with his head titled sideways and said, "Are you trying to use psychology, Mercer?"

"No!" I said politely. "You're my idol man, my neighbor who trained with me asked me to get your autograph for him if I ever had the chance to meet you."

Edwin looked doubtful. "Are you serious Mercer?" I said, "Yeah, for real man."

Moses signed it -- and then went on to win the race. I placed sixth, and with that finish, it ended the season. There is a lesson I must share with you about my experience in this event. Right before the start of this particular heat, as we approached the starting blocks, I heard John Francis, my coach from Butler Community College, give me a familiar tip. He said, "Mercer, don't look back." But of course, I couldn't resist: I actually had the lead at one point in the race, but then, despite knowing better and my coach's admonition, I looked back to check on where Moses was. I then had to stutter step due to losing my stride going into the eighth hurdle, and Edwin shot past me, drafting four other guys along with him. I finished the race in sixth place.

Today, I often have shared this fundamental aspect of competition with many athletes, because I know it probably made the difference for me in this race. Because I looked back for a split-second, I lost the only (however tenuous) opportunity to beat Edwin Moses.

(of course, he no doubt would have caught me anyway, in all honesty). I teach young athletes to respect their opponents, but during a race to stay focused on the finish-line, look straight ahead and always try to give your very best and finish strong. You may not always finish first, but the benchmark is to evaluate your success by doing better than you did before. This is the best sign of growth, development and maturity to be measured by any athlete.

I felt I should have placed much higher, but I lost focus. However, the experience was unforgettable and even though I lost that particular meet, I didn't lose available lessons because education was, and is the key. In the process of running the event of my life, in a single moment in time, I learned humility and character, while meeting a wonderful legend in sports, Mr. Edwin Moses.

During my years at Kansas State University, I had the pleasure of meeting a variety of very good people who became my friends.

I really did have a misconception about the people of Kansas. My early thoughts were formed by my ignorance and perhaps experience with other white and black southerners.

I thought they were just hillbillies, rednecks and slow, country black folks. I found that the vast majority of these people were kind-hearted, caring, and down to earth people who enjoyed life, laughter, agriculture and sports. The State of Kansas and its people have always been good to me. They represent some of the finest citizens in America. Without the proper education, both yesterday and today, I would likely be making misinformed decisions about people for the rest of my life. Education and people are the key. My pursuit of educational achievement allowed me to meet a gentleman named Darryl Anderson, who soon became a great friend. It is as if he were my brother.

Darryl played a critical role in my life at a time when I was in desperate need of some positive motivation and vision to believe that I could regain my academic eligibility at Kansas State.

I had been dismissed by K-State for poor academic performance issues and lost my full-scholarship. Darryl was one of my roommates and a great sprinter in track. As a runner-sprinter, in my opinion, he had one of the most explosive starts from the starting blocks anyone had ever seen. An injury to his thigh muscle later hampered his career, but did not stop his drive to excel in the classroom. Darryl encouraged me to spend more of my time in the library and utilize my peers who held study sessions.

Although I was a very quiet person in the classroom, I bought into his suggestions and strategy to utilize the vast resources available to me, including my academic advisors. Soon I was reinstated by the University, and from that day forward, my life changed for the better.

I had not spoken with Darryl for eight years when, in 1992, we made contact again. I asked him what was the biggest surprise he experienced in his career. Darryl replied, "You, Mercer. The biggest surprise was to see you graduate." You might remember that it was at these Olympic Games that Carl Lewis pursued a goal to establish a new World record by winning four Gold Medals, a feat which had only been accomplished prior, by Carl Lewis' idol, the great sprinter, Jesse Owens, during the 1936 Berlin Olympics. It was the meet in which Owens, an American Black man, demonstrated the fallacy of Hitler's Aryan superiority ideas. Then there was Al and Jackie Joyner, the dynamic brother and sister duo representing their hometown of East St. Louis, Illinois. Jackie Joyner was a very courageous athlete. Despite an injury to her leg, she was leading the other world competitors in the Heptathlon until, during the final event (the 800 meters), her injuries took their toll and she placed second by a mere 5 points.

All of these athletes displayed courage, courage to persevere, to not give up, to keep working and striving. Without that mindset, none of them could have succeeded in doing the remarkable things they accomplished.

GIVING BACK

Many of my greatest memories are in collegiate and professional sports. Getting an education and relying on smart people who were willing to be generous with their time and help were the keys that allowed me to work with many good and great athletes. I had the pleasure of coaching and encouraging Harry Butch Reynolds, a great track guy and former world record performer in the 1984 Olympic-Games from Ohio State University. His is a true story of resilience. I witnessed Harry running under 45 seconds in the 400 - meter run while in junior college. There was no way he was on steroids, but controversy surrounded him when he broke the world record. His brother Jeffrey, a Kansas State graduate, also ran 46 seconds and under, and he was clean as well. Today they are both civic leaders serving youth in their community of Akron, Ohio. I was involved in the young life of a 15-year old kid named Tai Streets.

Tai Streets is a very gifted athlete who played professional football for the San Francisco Forty-Niners and later the Detroit Lions. I really enjoyed the opportunity to be a part of his coaching, training and mentoring process. He was particularly special, because I made a promise to his mother to help him and his sisters to continue to strive for excellence in academics and sports. I made sure that they attended a series of clinics I sponsored, coordinated and conducted in 1992 called "The Gold Medal Summer Track Clinics."

The following fall semester I was a substitute teacher in one of his high school classes. I began to learn more about Tai Streets, a bright, talented young man with great potential and very good work habits and ethics for a young teenager. At this point Tai was a Freshmen in high school, and during my training sessions with him, I began to share with him all the knowledge I had gained. We began to discuss the finer techniques of being a great sprinter and the science of running.

I never had to repeat things to Tai because he had the ability to comprehend quickly and put it into action.

The results were almost immediate. Tai had a very good friend named Chris Blossom, who was a talented sprinter in his own right. Chris dominated high school level track and field until Tai entered the competitions. They began a good-natured battle for bragging rights during practices that made them both more competitive. Tai was a pure diamond in the rough, with the heart of a champion. He did whatever was asked of him; a coach's dream athlete. His backbone was nurtured by a strong and resilient mother.

Tai's mother was highly motivating and caring toward her children and other young people. She formed an AAU (Amateur Athletics) Track club for youth, which began with her own children participating. I got involved and supported her efforts by training and helping with fundraisers to raise money for her programs.

Mrs. Streets is a woman I really admire and respect, because she has experienced so much by way of challenges, struggles and a divorce, but despite everything, she held on to the reins and led her family on the road to achievement and success as best she could. Tai Streets continues to give back to many communities by offering his services in a variety of capacities, especially for the youth of America.

For years I have felt a deep discomfort or disappointment in myself for not wanting to have a closer association with some of the youth I helped along the way, due to my own downfalls. Most of them never knew the details before this book. Hopefully, it will give them greater insight and a better understanding of the Julius Mercer of yesterday and today. My hope is that this book will clear any pre-formed judgments they might have if they crossed my path during my troubled and turbulent years.

I hope and pray that someday, we will all cross paths again, and if this occurs, we may be able to forgive and help one another.

Education is the Key.

Every great act I have witnessed or experienced has come from people giving of themselves to others, or on behalf of an inspiration. Edwin Moses dedicated his performances in the 1984 Olympic Games to his Dad, and today I am writing my book and beginning my "**Contagious Visions**" in memory of, and dedication to my Dad.

PRIDE COMES BEFORE THE FALL

There are consequences to the decisions we make in life. Decisions we make can affect other people, including our family and even an entire community. I ventured down the road of life, thinking I was able to fix my problems by myself, and being afraid of what others might think: this was myself being full of pride. But in the end, this pride caused me to experience a painful fall that affected everyone in my life.

I broke a rule in my residential community that states, "Any person or persons who is charged and convicted of committing a felony is no longer allowed to live in this particular town-home condominium dwelling." Imagine if you will, my family had planted their roots there for over three decades. And now, because of my transgressions against humanity and myself, just to visit my own mother, sister and family at a place I once called home, I needed permission to prevent potential trespassing violations.

If I were to violate this residency ordinance, the property manager, the village management, and the police department would all have the option to evict my family from the town-home association and/or to have me arrested.

Prior to my distress, over many years I had developed a respectful relationship with the village management and police department. The village of Park Forest had once employed me as a summer part-timer to work with youth. In addition, Mr. John Joyce (now retired, then supervisor of recreation and parks) and Chuck Saby, who presently works with the town's music venue, helped launch the first Julius Mercer Gold Medal Summer Track Camp in 1992. They were a blessing to me and the community. I really enjoyed being in a position to inspire, challenge and assist in developing some of the finest young people through sports education, character – building, and life - skills as we circulated throughout the Village of Park Forest.

Perhaps the pay was not what I might have been able to earn doing other things; however, this was the least of my concerns.

My focus was to provide a safe, positive environment for the youth in my sphere of influence so they could have an alternative to loitering in the streets and getting into trouble. I worked tirelessly to positively influence the next generation: this is in fact one of my life's passions. We had lots of fun and I thank my dad for the words of wisdom he gave me during my youth and during my development working as a teacher's assistant in special education at Rich East High School in neighboring Richton Park. He said, "Son if any of your colleagues ever ask 'how is it that you are able to reach so many students that many of us gave up on,' just tell them, you're fair, open-minded and honest."

One day a Park Forest Police Officer told me, "Mercer, you make our job easier, because of all the time you've invested with these kids. "

Character is developed through action and footwork. Looking back at the time when my life was in chaos, I can remember the kindness of "Park Forest's Finest." There were several times that the police officers of Park Forest could have arrested me for minor transgressions, but instead they stopped me from harming myself and encouraged me to get some help for my issues of confusion, depression and helplessness.

There were a few times in my life when I witnessed some crooked cops whose behavior left a bad taste in my mouth, but I must admit that the officers of the Park Forest Police Department have left a positive impression on my heart.

A few of them are genuine in their efforts to execute their duties fairly and with justice. A respectful thank you to former Police Chief Robert Mae-yama. Under his leadership and on his watch, I was given every opportunity to get rehabilitated.

Of course, there were certain circumstances when they had to do more to calm down a guy who is 6"3 and weighs 225 lbs. Without hesitation, they put me in cuffs when I became a threat to others and myself. One officer once said to me, "It's for your own good." At the time, I thought to myself, how could being arrested and thrown into jail be for my own good? I now know he was right, though.

It wasn't until I had gone through detox that I became honest with myself. The detox process included forcing the drugs out of my system. I was treated medically for depression and then began to speak openly, honestly and thoroughly about every resentment, difference, negative experience and sorrowful feeling I was having.

I gave the uncut version to the professional therapists and psychiatrists, who listened to me without judgment and understood my anger and confusion. It was then that I really began to see that I had been rescued, not arrested.

Yes, I will admit many people tried to help me, but I didn't want their help, I didn't believe I needed their help, and I actually thought I could beat this on my own. I was wrong! Each time I attempted to help myself was an effort in vain. I sank deeper and deeper. This really baffled me because I was Julius Mercer, this champion athlete, who had overcome adversity and perhaps even greater odds on the track and field gridiron. As I became more educated about my particular form of depression, I began to recognize it was a false sense of pride bringing me down. Keep in mind that from a book sense, I was an educated and experienced social worker, servicing others who did not have practical and personal experience. I am not saying that for a social worker to be competent or successful one needs to go through what I did (as they say on TV: *please don't try this at home!*) but my experience took on a whole new meaning and made it real for me. I was then able to see and accept depression as a treatable illness.

The average person may not realize the depth of the internal mental and physical struggles. Even expert professionals are constantly discovering new problems associated with deep depression and are developing new approaches for the treatment and recovery of patients. False and negative pride can have us believing that us can just make up your mind and snap out of it. Once we have fallen too deeply, this thought process can be dangerous (an Illusion). An average level of mild depression or stress in our everyday lives can be managed and resolved when we talk with someone about what happened today, yesterday, or what is supposed to go on tomorrow. Another positive strategy is the use of positive ideas or changes that we rationally decide to make. Outlets like riding a bike, exercising, or taking on a new spontaneous adventure like boating, camping or concerts, movies and plays can be a source of new energy and inspiration. Meeting new people and sharing common experiences and ideas can also be refreshing.

Today, this has been and continues to be my daily pursuit. The new and improved Julius Mercer has found his vision and passion for a healthy, productive and wholesome life in harmony with others. I am extremely blessed to regain my health and sanity. My ability to conduct or handle myself in a reasonable manner had disappeared. Because I had reached a very serious level of manic depression, medical procedures became necessary to help me gain a sense of normalcy. I learned there are a lot of good and decent human beings who experience these things in their lives and never recover. They never regain their sanity and die with the disease. Doctors, lawyers, presidents, blue - collar or white - collar workers and other professionals may need some sort of assistance to maintain their sanity. No one is exempt from sorrow, tragedy, unexpected sudden death, loneliness, racial discrimination, or any number of other life situations that might send them over the edge. It all goes along with the journey of life.

I once told someone in an arrogant, unashamed manner that I would never become homeless, but there I was, full of pride. Depression, drugs, bad memories and pride had me living in the streets. I was spat upon and had raw eggs thrown at me. I was stigmatized and ridiculed.

Please allow me to share an important statistical note. A large majority of homeless people have at least two years of college education or have completed some type of pre-vocational training, and 25% are veterans of the armed forces. When a family or personal crisis hits, some people stray away in silence and this may be okay (just to get some time alone), so long as one can keep everything in perspective. Why is it that some people constantly feel insecure or question if where they are at in their life is wrong or not enough?

Why is it that some people are never is satisfied with who they are and unhappy with who they see in the mirror?

I've learned that pride comes before the fall!

Because of pride I began using crack cocaine, which began to adversely affect me; what had been good and healthy pride became, in me, overblown arrogance and confusion.

I thought I could maintain control over these substances and be okay. I was becoming immersed in drugs and uncharacteristic behaviors, and compounding my poor decision - making were a bunch of unresolved emotional issues.

Thank God for those Park Forest police officers who refused to give me a free pass. They did not discriminate or use my preferential celebrity status against me, but their duty was to serve and protect me from myself and others. They executed their responsibility and helped save my life.

Depression can trick anyone into believing that death is better than life. Someone once found me hanging from a pole by my own noose.

Even today, I often wonder who was that angel that pulled me down and called the paramedics. My depression led to three suicide attempts, which, according to the law in some states, is a felony in some cases. I actually do not even remember these suicide attempts, and when I awoke in the hospitals and was told about it by the doctors, I was in total denial. "Not me, not Julius Mercer. Julius Mercer would never try to take his own life." The doctors then went on to explain that I reacted this way because I was not in my right mind.

They continued to explain how important it was for me to talk about these issues that were bothering me and not hold in the anger. Perhaps had I not allowed this pride of self-treatment to hold me back from seeking competent help, much of my mental distress and related criminal actions might have been avoided.

DEPRESSION AND MENTAL ILLNESS

My negative outlook on life took shape soon after my divorce. When my former wife removed herself and our daughter away, I felt guilty because my parents were being denied a relationship with their granddaughter. This dwelling on the negative was one more finger pulling the trigger which exploded into a deep depression. My Mother and sister Robin were the first to sense that something was going wrong with me. This type of discernment is probably the greatest gift of the Mercer women. Then my father followed the clues and his "gut-feeling" told him to convince me to enter a hospital for manic depression. I was admitted into the Tinley Park Mental Treatment Center in Tinley Park, Illinois, where I was under close supervision for eight days. The biggest mystery to me at the time was: when I came to my right mind, thanks to the medical professionals and the appropriate medication, I had no memory of how I had arrived there.

My father, in his foresight and wisdom, had persuaded me to pursue this course of action even while I was literally in a manic state of mind. On the eighth day at Tinley Park, I looked around my surroundings and noticed that I was surrounded by people with obvious serious mental illnesses. I didn't know how I had gotten there, but assumed that I was a social worker, there to help these people. I saw across the hallway, into another room, a security guard, so I tried to open the door from my room, but I was unable to get it open. I pounded on the door and yelled at him that I was not one of the patients, I was actually an employee. He, in turn, ordered me to "sit your ass down."

"Oh no!" I thought, "how could this be?" The officer once again yelled, "sit your crazy (bleep~) down before I give you a shot."

In my delusion, I actually thought I had a new job because when I looked out the windows, I recognized where I was: Harlem Ave near I-80.

I began to cry profusely in a mass of confusion, wondering how this could have ever happened to me. I began to pray and ask God for forgiveness for any and everything I had ever said to belittle anyone or hurt anyone's feelings. I now realize that something was wrong with me but at the time I did not understand anything. I only believed that seeking pleasurable things would make me feel better. Again, pride would not allow me to face this head on. The false pleasures of the drugs were temporary, and I actually always felt much worse afterwards.

I had become an habitual liar and wore a mask of deception that injured my deepest relationships. I could not stay at home around my family, particularly my parents, whom I loved dearly, and did not want to expose to them my weaknesses or failures. I would be careful to be sober around the immediate family. A silent destroyer was creeping into my life, a mentally crippling force.

I later learned that even my brothers Fred and Mike joined the family in prayers for me to get better while offering encouragement. My family's quiet and persistent support proved to me our family's love for one another.

I have learned that majority of people have had, or will at some point have, unresolved issues in their life. We all do. But sometimes, and with some people, these issues can become overpowering, weakening our ability to fully function. It may not be our fault, but we do have resources to use our power to take control of our lives back and into a new direction. Road rage or other irritations that begin small but careen into larger events can be the symptoms that, if left untreated, can have a major impact on society. Now, whenever I notice my thinking becoming negative or I am becoming overly critical of others.

I am learning to recognize it and how these negative thoughts affect me in a bad way, and I try to instead think about that other person as a complete individual, with his or her own fears and thoughts.

Determination and perseverance, when focused in the right direction, are very powerful forces within a person. Winston Churchill said, *"Don't give up, don't give up, don't ever quit!"* It took me a long time to get it right. Many of my close friends thought I would never get back to my normal self. But as bad as things seemed, and as much as I repeated bad habits, I knew in my heart that someday, somehow, I was going to have a major breakthrough. Once the breakthrough happened, I knew I could do something special to assist others.

In 1984, I placed third in the United States Track and Field Championships 400-meter hurdles in Houston, Texas. My track coach, Steve Miller, gave me a tool to increase my confidence: visualization.

He asked me to close my eyes and see the race unfolding, and see myself easily clearing the hurdles in the lead, and see myself winning the race.

As a college freshmen and sophomore at Butler Community College, I earned the honor of being a four–time All-American by finishing in the top three places in both the indoor and outdoor National Championship meets. Coach John Francis laid the foundation of strength, speed and endurance through his great training routines. He was able to shift my nervousness or paradigm of thought that was limiting my improvement. As a result, at the end of the final race, I placed 3rd, winning a bronze medal. Not a bad accomplishment for a kid who entered the race with the second-best qualifying time.

Another wonderful thing occurred, the ASICS Tiger Shoe Manufacturing Company became my sponsor, and the more I believed that I could do better, the more amazing things happened.

I put all my energy into improving and went on to qualify for the Olympic trials (*Track and Field News* predicted I had an outside chance to make the team) held at the United States Track and Field Championships in Indianapolis, Indiana (I placed 6th).

Immediately following the Championships, I was chosen to represent the U.S. at the World University Games that following July in Edmonton, Canada. Being on the international traveling team was a huge honor for me. I traveled and competed in several states and Japan. I had the honor of meeting Prince Charles and Lady Diana, our hosts in Canada.

My former Coach, Mr. Steve Miller, was an expert at not allowing negative thinking to take over my state of mind. One night, we were driving back from a meet in Iowa in the team van. The other athletes were asleep, so I and Coach Miller took the opportunity to discuss anything that came to mind. One thing he said to me was, "Life is full of moments."

I have often recalled that, as a warning to always be aware of our little opportunities take advantage of all that life offers. Recently, for example, I was at a concert and noticed Chicago's mayor Emanuel sitting behind me. Rather than be nonchalant about it, I took advantage of the moment and went over to him and talked for several minutes. Why not?

Determination seems to be a common theme; a central key for people who become healthy, wealthy and wise. They focus on solutions.

I recall a conversation with my former high school track – and - field coach shortly after my college graduation. I wanted to know why he had not encouraged me to attend college or further my education, even though I'd won so many trophies and ribbons while competing for his teams.

(At one point I was ranked in the top five of Illinois State High School Hurdlers.)

His surprising and discouraging answer was, "I'm sorry Julius, I didn't think that you could handle the college level classes." I was hurt and felt insulted.

This instance illustrated for me the issue many black athletes face: there is often a presumption that they are incapable to rising to the challenge of college. This is one reason why many gifted black athletes never reach their full potential.

Although I was bitter from not being encouraged to attend college, I still have respect for the opportunities and position that my coach gave me. What bothered me the most was that I came from a string of Mercer brothers: Mike, Fred and Chris. Upon Dad's retirement from 23 years in the Army, our family moved to Park Forest from Newport News, Virginia in 1973. During this time, you could count the number of black people in Park Forest on two hands. We faced racial slurs and confrontations.

It was worse for my brothers Fred and Mike, as they were older. Things had gotten so bad for them that the constant anger distracted them from discovering their true potential. Dad encouraged them to join the Army, so they dropped out of school and enlisted in the armed forces. Fred and Mike had set high school track records in both running and jumping events. While serving in the Army during the 80s, Fred became an outstanding 400-meter hurdler with a personal best time two tenths faster than my best when I was world class status. Mike was one of the best sprinters and could run 200 meters in 20.88, and 100 meters in 10.35 seconds bare-footed. Imagine had Fred and Mike had the advanced technical access and coaching I had. My brother Chris participated on a state qualifying relay team.

The Mercers, Davis and Hicks (Mom's maiden name) have produced many great athletes from Tennessee and Texas.

I am proud to be an alumnus of Rich East High School in Park Forest. Despite some tough economic times, it was and remains a good school. The support from the dedicated teachers and the rest of the local community had a positive impact on my life.

There were so many others within our family with tremendous successes: Ray Mercer was a 1996 Olympic Goals medal boxer; Candice and Janice Mercer were star track athletes at Evanston Township High School and my cousin, Johnny Lee Jackson, was inducted in the Mineral Wells High School Hall of Fame in 2009.

The Chicago Sun-Times published an article on my high school, focusing on its famous alumni and most memorable athletic events throughout its history. All of my friends were mentioned – but I was not. As you can imagine, resentment tore me apart; this resentment grew within me until the anger was almost unmanageable.

I have never allowed anger to lead me to violence; thank goodness I have had really good therapists who worked with me on not letting this negative thinking get the best of me.

Two of the best therapists I have had are Crystal Hreska and Kadija Alaka, of the Trilogy Family Mental Health Services of Chicago. Therapy has taught me to let go of resentment. The key, for me, was to forgive myself and others. This was extremely difficult to do.

How did I forgive myself? First, I recalled the things I did, that I know I shouldn't have done to myself or others. I then was able to focus how those acts or omissions caused harm to myself or others.

I do this still today. After recalling and understanding what I did that I should not have done, I then pray, admitting my failures, lamenting the harm I have caused, and asking for forgiveness.

Even in the days I was not feeling especially spiritual, I still found the need to say a simple phrase out loud: , "I forgive myself and I forgive others," and then I was able to go forward with my life.

It takes a very brave person to admit to themselves or to others that he or she is wrong but I found it brings me an inner calm, a sense of freedom and peace. Afterwards, I am better able to avoid the same mistakes (of course, I continually fail also ... that is part of life's journey and I accept my failures and my attempts at improvement as two sides of the same coin of the realm, the price of living. I no longer beat myself up for any of it.)

I have had many set-backs and even emotional failures in my life. There is much I am not proud of in my past. However, I smile today with pride, knowing that as of 2019, I still hold records in track and field at Kansas State University and Rich East High School high school.

I hold the number one spot, a record for the men's 300 low hurdles at Rich East high school and the men's 400-meter hurdles at Kansas State University, as well as the third fastest time in the men's 110-meter hurdles at K-State.

I FIGHT MY INNER DEMONS

When my divorce was followed so shortly by my father's death I immediately began feeling sorry for myself, which caused a complete emotional reversal. I reacted with angry outbursts and an "I don't care anymore" attitude, began drinking alcohol excessively and using hard drugs, and got involved with others who using and selling drugs. I was not just hurting myself: I was also hurting the people who cared about me the most. I now know that my drowning in this maelstrom which led to my three suicide attempts wasn't a display of weakness, but rather a scream that I was hurting. The desire to end one's own life can happen to anyone who keeps angry, negative feelings bottled up inside. These feelings can explode under a variety of circumstances; with me, circumstances included experiencing a divorce and death of a parent closely together, but it could just as easily have been anything negative that would have left me feeling overwhelmed.

I have learned psychological tools which I – or anyone – can use: when I am feeling overwhelmed, I have a series of steps that I take. First, I stop what I'm doing and remain still so I can think. Then, I make it a point to only do the most important things to the exclusion of all else. I have found that once I have completed one or two important things, my brain begins to register order. This allows me to continue slowing myself down by reminding myself that I am not a machine, but a faulty human being. Then I begin to realize that I'm back in control.

Our self-esteem is how we feel about ourselves; therefore, I needed to take actions to regain my forward progress. I needed to develop a system of self-motivation. It takes practice to stop thinking negatively.

It bothered me for years that my mental illness negatively affected my decision-making process. This illness had me continuously putting myself in precarious positions.

I would have never dreamed of being in situations like warming-up in an abandoned building, sleeping overnight on a cold dirty warehouse floor, riding the Chicago trains until the early morning, sleeping in wrecked cars that were towed to automotive shops, befriending people just so I could snatch money from their hands and run.

These inappropriate behaviors became extremely common occurrences, but were not unique to me. Substance abusers and alcoholics share syndromes such as domestic violence, blackouts, being argumentative, living in the streets, lacking the ability to control impulses, belittling or tearing down the self-esteem of others and self, and needing to constantly have a drink to settle the shaking hands

If we would take the time to think about all the good or positive that can happen, even if the good seems a little farfetched, we could make the needed changes.

Then we could regain the process of taking a major step to change our direction in order to avoid the pitfalls. If I had to pick one thing that ultimately put me on a stronger and more committed path to change, it would be that I wasn't happy with the way my life was going. In other words, my belief and the ways I envisioned myself living was in conflict with my reality. Yes, there was some pressure from my family and friends, but the biggest pressure was self-inflicted, due to my not living up to my own standards. To change, I had to learn to recognize the negative influences in my life, those emotional or mental attacks which were slowing me down, then I was able to see the links between those negative concepts and my pain. I had to make some changes with my belief system. I now turn negative situations such as a misunderstanding or a feeling of being disrespected into a self-motivating game.

I redirect the internal conflict or anxiety I feel from a negative situation into a goal-oriented experience that I use to motivate myself. This allows me the opportunity to utilize self-motivation and drive in order to help myself. However, the attitude must be focused on change for the better. Once I learned this, I began to set goals and reprioritize my values. Once, in prison, an inmate gave me a couple of self-help books; once I realized this process of enabling myself to improve, I was able to study these books more seriously.

Today, I attend Therapeutic Cognitive support group three times a week for 12 months at Trilogy Behavior Mental Health Services in Chicago, learning that I don't know everything, and learning how to treat others less fortunate than I with respect and unconditional love. My bad attitude, anger, and inability to forgive others and myself, allowed negative spiritual forces to dominate and have power over me.

When I gave up my power to make the right choices for my mental health and well-being, I basically gave the reins to the negative spiritual power in my life.

It is my belief that when I treat myself or others badly then that negativity will come back to me in some way or another. This is my form of Karma. Yes, I treated my family, friends and people who attempted to help me badly, but nothing can compare to the way I treated myself. I was put out of half-way homes and slept in abandoned buildings, not realizing that I was sleeping on other people's defecation and urine. The scurrying sounds of huge rats roaming throughout the night, looking for food, kept me from sleeping.

I walked miles and miles, hustling up money to keep my high going. Leg cramps and blisters had me resting on strangers' porches, in hallways, and many times on park benches. I fell asleep overnight in parks and when I woke up, birds would run and I'm sure they were chirping, "that dead man woke-up."

Once I was so thirsty, I mistakenly drank urine from a pop bottle someone had tossed in an abandoned building. Twice I slept in cardboard boxes, once in my dress clothes and a necktie (I had had a job interview earlier that day) and often in abandoned buildings. I was cold, lonely, scared, hungry and depressed.

All addictions have something in common: a compulsion to repeat the behavior that started after the first series of drinks and hits, or the first chips in a bag, or a bowl of ice cream, cake, or that first roll of the dice. Whatever the addiction, we just can't seem to stop. I have overcome problems and obstacles and been able to achieve and accomplish things because I found joy or something positive to focus on. My pain level had finally reached such an intensity that my brain said, "No more! Enough of this unhealthy living, I'm tired of feeling this way."

Now, every day, to stay positive, and experience the same natural feelings of pleasure, I no longer look to drugs or alcohol; I use laughter, jogging, weight lifting, prayer, and other physical activity and recreational sports. I post "sticky notes" with positive affirmations on them around my apartment. Sometimes a good conversation with friends works as well. I once believed I was too strong to be broken by hard drugs (there's that pride again!). I now know how terribly wrong I was, and I've learned and found avenues to avoid travelling again that destructive road. I always had a desire to help others, and had worked with teens, and I've discovered that helping others gives me a tremendous feeling. However, as I recovered, I had to ask myself "How can I begin to help others when my personal issues are still hounding me?" I met the most inspirational man when I was incarcerated. He was in his late thirties and sentenced to forty years for a string of armed robberies. He was initially sentenced to life in prison without the possibility of parole.

We both attended weekly group support meetings that focused on cognitive changes. At one point he was filled with so much guilt and confusion that he ended up being hospitalized for suicidal tendencies.

Then, when he was released from the hospital and sent back to the general population and our group sessions, an amazing thing began to happen. He shared with the group how he believed the Spirit of God wouldn't allow him to follow through with killing himself. His testimony reached the hearts of everyone in attendance. It even had me crying. These were tears of relief, knowing that everything was going to be all right. He inspired all of us, saying, "Just because we have an X on our backs, doesn't mean that we are X'd out of everything." I thought to myself, "this is a good brother." He was trying to fight off issues all by himself, just like I was. Neither of us had planned to become a menace to society. We both knew we were out of control and destroying other lives, including our own families.

We were both hurting badly and didn't know how to handle it. Yes, I was taught to "man-up" and handle situations like a man; dry up those tears and get busy. If I had been able to stop the monster early, I would have had a fighting chance to avoid all of this, but by now society's menace had become full – blown, and it had been entirely due to my inability to be honest with myself and reach out and grab the waving hands of those who tried to help me. If I didn't make cognitive changes, then my family and children would continue to be hurt by my actions.

How do I get these problems out of my head? How do I change these feelings from bad to good? A technique I learned to use is "Peak Performance." The motivational author, Anthony Robbins, teaches people how to formulate questions that will empower an individual to think differently. He encourages all his readers to share his materials with others, so I will do so: One of his exercises is this: I want you to think of a problem that bothers you right this moment.

For example, something that bothered me for years was why my dad never attended any of my high school sporting events. The most hurtful memory was when my high school held "Parent's Night" honors for each athlete's parents. Every one of my basketball teammates' parents showed up, but not my dad. Dad had told me earlier in the day, "we'll see, son." I explained to him that mom wanted to go. When Dad didn't show and only Mom did, I became angry and held on to the resentment.

What I learned is that I had a control problem. If other people did not act like I wanted them to or if they did not follow my rules, even when it related to affection and its reciprocity, I would become angry. Therapeutic support classes at Circle Family Services of Chicago has well-educated psychiatric professionals who helped me understand my control issues, including the harmful effects and emotional impact it was wreaking on me and my loved ones.

The fact is that we cannot change or control anyone's response to anything. However, we can take control of how *we* respond to a given situation. We can hope, pray, encourage or suggest, but trying to control another's decisions can destroy the natural innate spirit called love. So I asked myself, "Why do you want to have control?"

I then realized it was so I could control my feelings of pain or pleasure that resulted from people doing what I wanted them to do.

Now I can see how important values are. They are the real compass to provide direction in my life – in all our lives. I used hypothetical role-playing to assist me. I would make up a situation, and reflect on my past reaction to this crisis. I would then think through the appropriate action and store it in my memory. Also, a big part of my reasoning was evaluating my reaction to other peoples' crisis. I would use empathy, openness, honesty, listening and support to help stabilize them.

However, I could not support myself when a major crisis, like a family member dying in my arms, hit me.

In some cases, the only thing any of us may be able to do in a mental or medical crisis is provide a hug, hold a hand, and let them know you are there if they need to talk, get a cold wet towel and apply pressure to the wounded area until help arrives, dial 911, or just hope and pray. I have learned the hard way that abusing alcohol or the misuse of drugs during a crisis is not the answer. It took a long time to see it, but of course every time my buzz wore off, my problems were still there.

For some strange reason there are still times when the idea of using drugs runs through my mind. Therapists have helped me by explaining that since I sought pleasure through a combination of drugs and sex, I may subconsciously continue to have these thoughts and desires for several months or possibly years.

I have spoken with other men who quit using hard drugs or have abstained from alcohol for several years and they've said at times, they were still fighting off thoughts and dreams about relapsing into their destructive past actions; this even after 20 years of abstinence.

For a long time after I began my abstinence from drugs, I would still often look into cars as I walked past, almost as an impulse, or a habit I couldn't break, to think of what was in there to steal. Fortunately, this habit and these thoughts have now long ago disappeared, with the help of a lot of therapy, prayer, and positive encouragement. A child has to be guided through their youth and teen years. A child learns adult behaviour from the model of the adults in his or her life. Therefore, if a child's parents or guardians are teaching and role modeling negative actions, attitudes and behaviours, then it is likely that the child will see that as "the way adults behave," and will have problems relating positively to society.

I believe that many of us don't have a drinking problem, drug problem, or a weight problem; instead we have a values problem. Negative, destructive behaviors can happen because of anger and frustration, self-doubt or insecurity. Again, I had to learn to ask myself questions that helped take me out of my depression. Some of the questions I still must face are:

a.   Do I worry too much?

b.   Why do I doubt myself so much?

c.   Am I a worthy person?

d.   What is the source of my stress?

e.   Am I creating my own anxiety?

f.   That is the reason I am angry?

g.   Am I doing everything I can to help?

e.   Can my counselors help me?

Questioning myself, I found, helps me regain direction and consciousness; the process leads me to the source of my frustration or confusion.

When I want to laugh to keep from crying, I may lift up my arm and kick my legs from side to side while singing a happy song.

So if you see me dancing and singing "I represent the Lollipop Guild, the Lollipop Guild, the Lollipop Guild ...," (from *Wizard of Oz*[2]) you will know what I'm doing!

---

[2] *Wizard of Oz,* music by Harold Arlen, lyrics by E.Y. Harburg.

My senior year at Rich East H.S. Starting forward.

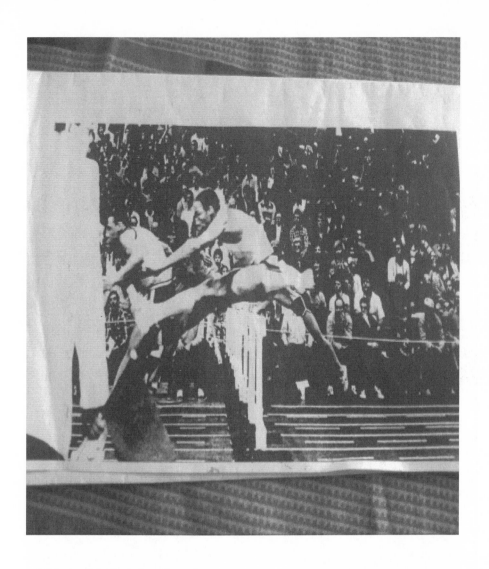

1981, NJCAA, finals

Courtesy, Empowering Athletes For Life,
Rockford, Illinois, 2019'

Courtesy, Hyatt Elementary School,

'Career Day', 2018

Julius Mercer launches, Contagious Visions'
anti-bully educational platform, 2019'

THOUGHTS OF PRISON

Prison is no place for anyone. I was a "guest of the state" four different times, and each one was more emasculating and dehumanizing than the last. (A small story: when I entered prison for my last visit, one prison official told me: "Mercer, we've had a lot of high-profile gang leaders here, but you are the highest profile athlete we've ever had." At first, I felt kind of complimented, but that soon changed to "this sucks!") There were many sleepless nights filled with the sounds of sexual abuse. I learned to carry myself in a certain way to avoid being sexually assaulted in prison by the gangs. When approached, I would become fighting mad, and start using profane language while threatening them. I had at least three fights and a handful of confrontations with gang members, all because I wasn't a member. I had not fought too much growing up. In fact, the last fight I recall was at the age of 12. And here I was now, fighting for my life at 36, 40, and 43 years of age.

When I initially arrived at prison, I weighed 185 lbs. While there, I committed myself to a rigorous regimen of weightlifting, running and jumping rope. Within months I swelled up to 225 natural pounds of muscle to enable me to defend myself against physical pressure and intimidation.

As a result, several gang members made failed attempts to get me to join their groups. They all began to call me "Red-dogg" a nickname given to me by the "Latin Folk" – gang members. Everywhere I went they called me "Red-dogg." I took on the name and demeanor, and that's how I survived in a pit filled with animalistic behavior. I exhibited animal-like behavior when the circumstances called for it.

There were some gang members who wanted to change, to leave the "gangster" life behind and lead real life outside the prison system, but the pressure to run with the gangs almost always overcame such desire for change. It's important for me today to make smart decision-making a higher priority on my list of values.

Poor decisions have put me in situations where I've had to adapt and adjust to survive. I conformed to the peer pressures and allowed them to change me into an insecure, isolated, distrustful, always-on-the-edge type of man. If this could happen to me in such a short period of time, then imagine the affect it has on 90% of those incarcerated, who began experiencing these pressures from infancy through adulthood. Incarceration in a "correctional institution" doesn't "correct" the individual; treatment, ongoing therapy and, often, a total psychiatric overhaul are needed.

There are approximately 30 prisons in the State of Illinois and less than half of them have a substance abuse program. There are those who deserve to be locked up and put away. I deserved every consequence that I had coming; however, having access to rehabilitative programs, even after repeating the offenses, was the key to helping me break the cycle.

Eli, a prisoner, serves as a constant example to me. Eli's bad decisions led him to a maximum-security prison. He often shared with me how much he wanted to get out and be a better father to his son, whom he was afraid was following in Eli's footsteps of crime. Ironically and tragically, within a year, Eli was sharing a cell with his son, who had been arrested and found guilty of murder. I saw in Eli's eyes how much this deeply hurt his heart, mind and soul. He stayed confused and depressed for several years, but because he never sought a continuous support system, he suffered silently and remained in a depressed mode that he just couldn't shake. This deep depression locked up his mind and kept him constantly handcuffed and a prisoner – of the state and of his own mind.

When I was a kid, a famous comedian named Bill Cosby created a cartoon show called, "Fat Albert and The Cosby Kids." The main character was Fat Albert an overweight African-American man with large protruding lips.

There was another African-American male character with extra-large protruding lips that would bump together when he spoke. His name was Mush-mouth and his pronunciation of letters and words would echo double sounds. Everyone would laugh at him.

I came from a family of African-American males with large lips. After the very first Saturday morning episode back in 1972, many kids teased me by calling me the Cosby Kid. It hurt my feelings so much because it was my own African-American brothers and sisters making fun of me. I took more abuse from them than I did from white people. I became angry and often cried. For years I wasn't happy with the way I looked, but all of that changed one day when an African-American teacher visited my prison during Kwanzaa told me to be proud because my lips identified my African heritage and ancestry. She told me to visualize my "name in lights."

This woman was the first person to ever tell me I needn't be ashamed of my looks, but should be proud of how I looked.

Ninety-percent of inmates in prison grow up without a mom or dad due to death or the mom or dad being incarcerated. Many of their parents were substance abusers who suffered from a mental illness. I would say that 80% of those I met in jail or prison had no high school diploma and had difficulty reading and writing. The recidivism rate for repeat offenders is close to 80%.

After the Emancipation Proclamation was put in place, many former slaves were given a few clothing items and enough food for a few days. But they were uneducated, illiterate and unskilled, and therefore at the mercy of local farmers and sharecroppers. Many farmers had discovered a market for cheap labor, paying very little wages and in some cases only providing clothing and housing.

The prison system of today is not that much different. I traveled to four different prisons. The pay was $15 a month for a job which was normally a $10 an hour job and $40 - $60 dollar per month for what would have been a $1,200 monthly job in regular society. The majority of the products produced by prisoners include poultry and bakery items which are sold at markets throughout the country. Some inmates use their money to pay for protection to keep from being sexually abused. I never had that problem, because when I first went to prison, a correctional officer who worked at a local courthouse instructed me to abide by three rules. "1). Be careful who you talk to 2). Be careful what you say 3). Don't mess with the "sissies." Those were his exact words and I followed them each and every day I was in prison. I heard many sounds of sexual escapades and abuses, and I was surprised to see many prisoners who I thought were trustworthy were some of the most frightful abusers in the darkness.

Fighting is very common in jails and prisons. Many people have been stabbed and killed with a shank (knife). Shanks are metal or steel pieces that have been shaved to make a pointed sharp edge. I've seen many prisoners get what is called "pumpkin heads" by being repeatedly beaten on their heads with a sock filled with canned goods. These individuals were hit so often that it caused swelling of the brain. The swelling is so acute that the person's head looks like a pumpkin. I had a lot of lessons to learn in order to survive as peacefully as possible. The most important thing was to try and not resolve a confrontation or problem by fighting someone who belongs to a gang, even if they were the instigators. I had three physical fights while in prison. I was challenged because my demeanor was that of an easy-going, nice guy, non-gang member, non-member of anything. A non-member was called a neutron, meaning neutral, with no affiliations to any mob organization.

I never had problems with the gang members 35 and older. It was mostly those who were 18-30 that seemed to have a chip on their shoulders. They were opportunists. always seeking out whom they could devour. Usually they tried to be slick, be it a card game of trickery, or taxing a person for not paying back money they borrowed.

I have never claimed to be a fighter; however, during my time there I was occasionally challenged by these young "tough guys." When that happened, my "Smoking Joe Frazier" came out (I am 6-4 and remember I was weighing 225 of muscle) and, after I set a couple of them straight – in a language they could understand -- I didn't have any problems thereafter. In fact, some members made attempts to recruit me afterwards. I grew pretty close to the elder mob leaders because of my athleticism in all the prison activities including baseball, softball, track, ping-pong, volleyball and basketball. Prison inmates are really big on sports and very competitive.

When they found out I was a former world-class athlete, the gang's shot callers (big bosses) would put out a protective tent over me to ensure that other members wouldn't start any trouble with me. They also explained to me that if any member gave me any trouble, I should notify their superiors, and as long as I did this, I would avoid gang hits. The instigators would receive a gang-issued "violation."

The fourth and final time I was incarcerated was different. I began to associate incarceration with pain. The food was painful, the beds, the lights, seeing the barbed-wired fences, the officers, the chairs, the holidays away from family and friends, and the loss of ability to do something positive. Everything had become extremely painful for me. My mindset prior to my arrest would tell me: I can do this, it's nothing, I've done it before.

I relapsed so easily; my mental reasoning was deficient. I could not view and understand the world in a rational manner.

As Anthony Robbins would write, I had not experienced sufficiently the reward differences between pain and pleasure. I really did not understand (actually could not imagine) how much more pleasure there would be for me if I were to discard my old life. I was blind to the benefits of change. Even when I was put in the county jail (which I was 16 times, by the way), my first thought was not "this is bad, this is wrong, I can do better with my life," but rather, it was "oh, this is okay. I'll go the psych ward and it'll be fine."

This was, I now know, the lingering effects of my psychotic breakdown of 20 years before, following my divorce and my father's death and the culture shock of moving from bucolic Kansas to the darkness of Los Angeles. However, it was also tied to the feeling of rejection I had bottled up, untreated over many years.

Many people can't see the benefit in changing. When I began to make small changes, I immediately experienced small successes and, recognizing these successes, enabled me to establish some momentum to continue on a positive path.

My capacity for positive emotional responses to life grew stronger and stronger. Positive spiritual energy and responses began to come naturally. One example that helps explain this might be:

A basketball team is down by 10 points with under 4 minutes to play. One player hits a "3," and then another player makes a steal.

Suddenly the entire team catches this spiritual energy, even the fans. The noise becomes overwhelming for the other team's players, who throw the ball away and miss open shots. The energy, the spirit of positivity that began with one small spark ended up catching the entire arena on fire, leading to a big victory over a rival.

This is just an example, but the point is: I know that we are all able to overcome the emotional vacuum we often find ourselves. Help is needed, and help is available. It is when people don't get help to face their painful memories that it becomes difficult for them to overcome negative emotional quicksand. With the right processes, all of us are able to move forward once we have faced the past.

THE ROAD TAKEN

All of us go through a period where we have to survive peer pressure and make smart choices; I certainly did. Both negative and positive peer pressure has affected me and my happiness. I lived most of my life being controlled by others, and when I tried to control others, it really meant that I had no control over myself. During one of my counseling sessions while moving toward recovery, I was told that I was somewhat controlling. I left, asking myself "How did I become this way?"

As part of my training to become a social worker, I learned the theory that behaviors are learned and many males and females suffer from central issues. For me, learning how to be controlling came from my father. During my teen years, my dad insisted we all conform our conduct and our thought patterns to his, and if we deviated, he got angry with us for the display of independence.

In this book to this point, you have read of behavioral issues I experienced as a child, and not once did I blame my actions on the drugs or alcohol to be part of the problem. Substance abuse and depression were the end results, not the causes. My main problem was obsessive compulsive disorder, along with entertaining negative thoughts which were triggered by my dad's habits of always wanting his way.

I now know why I relapsed so easily. In my mind, I did not associate drugs, alcohol and a dissipated life with pain. I saw no real reason to change.

When I finally began to make small changes, the initial small steps gave me the positive momentum to continue on the new positive path. My capacity to love grew stronger and stronger. My spirits came back to me.

I had suffered silently because I had been afraid to show my real self to those who loved and cared for me. I didn't share my feeling of confusion, hurt and anger.

When people told me "you'll be all right, man-up, just forget about it, it will pass," I should have taken immediate action, but instead I just sat back and just wished for it all to go away.

I now know how that *wishing* for my problems to disappear couldn't get it done. I learned I could control these problems, and I actually had the power to get these out of my life.

How? By changing my habits. I wrote up a list of values. I now know that the way to become better educated is by asking questions (I flunked out of "being quiet.") Too often I went around saying "I can't change; this is who I am, it is in my blood."

I once read in a book: "If you were told that you have only two days to live, what would you change in the world?"

We all have a special gift of Free Will (Choice). The habits, rituals, and routines we all have were learned, sometimes far back our distant past. I learned in prison that the tougher I got, the more the gangs wanted me to join them.

As I said in earlier chapters, the majority of people in prison are not necessarily bad people. Ninety percent grew up with no real family life. Either their mom or dad died, or their mother had multiple babies coming from several men. The mom and/or dad were often alcoholics, drug users, or physical abusers who were themselves abused. They have seen close friends get killed by gunfire. For a child, these types of experiences greatly impact emotional stability. These influential social traumas went untreated.

It isn't easy changing habits, but it can be done. Bad habits come in many forms. Some of them we may not see as negative but they are: drinking too much, over-reacting, controlling others, being perpetually late, or even always being in a hurry. As a child I developed some inappropriate sexual habits that were taught to me by other kids, I thank God that these negative habits did not last. Giving up, negative thinking, not talking about problems, complaining, hanging around people who caused trouble or got into trouble, procrastinating, these are all habits which happen to people who are angry or feel empty inside, and I had many of them. They led to confusion and doubting my own worth.

So my first step to abate confusion was to become aware that I had choices. I developed a system to avoid confusion: I begin by listing possible solutions or outcomes to the situation or circumstance that requires a decision. I then select the one outcome which seems likely to become the most beneficial to me and make a decision to work toward the desired outcome.

Thomas Edison tried 9,999 times to invent the light bulb. Someone asked him "are you going to fail 10,000 times?" Mr. Edison said, "I've never failed. I've learned 9,999 ways not to make a light bulb."

During my senior year in high school, I was confused. I was the number one hurdler and I saw no future. When I had a 1.65 grade point average, I knew I had to change.

I sought out tutors and students who helped me get it up to a 2.5 G.P.A. and I managed to graduate. I had to change. Today I still demand more for myself. I challenge myself in all circumstances to believe I can do it!

The most powerful tool for change is belief. When I say "I can do it," I gain power. Belief tells me what is possible and what is impossible. What we believe is the compass and map that guides us towards our goals.

I was born with something wrong with my leg and, as a result, I wore leg braces as a child. No one ever knew that I would become an Olympic competitor, but something powerful was in me. I loved running, and when we love something, we have the foundation for the necessary tools of success: determination and persistence. When I was getting C's, D's or F's in school, I needed to change my actions.

The only person who was able to control my destiny or future was me! Being certain causes power.

Before 1954, no one was able to run a mile faster than four minutes. Then, on May 6, 1954, Roger Bannister walked onto a track at Oxford University, confident and certain he could run the mile in under 4 minutes. He did it (making headlines the world over), and that show of strength opened the doors wide to where, as of 2019 over 1,400 people have run under four minutes! The lesson I take from this is that with confidence, I could make a lasting change in my life and that when any of us makes a positive change in our lives, it affects many, many other people. We might not break the mile record, or make changes we can see over the entire world, but we can cause a ripple, and even the smallest ripple pushes all the water around it to changes.

We as human beings are not gangsters, bad people, liars or a bunch of dummies, despite what we are often told. We are glorious creations with unlimited potential!

Each of us is a solution for someone. Someone told me that if I could make someone smile or laugh, offer a shoulder to a holding hand; if I could go even farther and maybe help cancer patients, feed the poor, or help old people, then I would be a hero.

When I was trying to recover and cut loose from the pull of drugs and alcohol, I used to say "I am a drug addict." Now I say "I'm a health nut."

I work with and give talks to students; I spend my time trying to be a solution for someone. I have completely changed my identity. I used to think math was too hard. I'd say to myself, "I'm stupid." I changed my identity, to where I now say, "I'm smart and if I work at it, I can solve this problem." I just had to find another way to figure it out.

Whenever something happens in my life my brain asks two questions: pain or pleasure? By changing my attitude and twisting my mind around to where I am thinking positively, my whole life changed.

Thinking positively meant that I know that everything that happens to me now will help me improve in some way.

Any of us can be a hero. I needed to begin with me: change my life decisions, so I could be a hero to myself. I was then able to see myself as someone who could be funny, be crazy, have fun, maybe even take chances on success. But the main thing was that I learned from my many (many, many) mistakes in life. It was all only a series of lessons, so I realized I didn't need to be perfect. For every problem, I spent time finding the reason for the problem, and then jettisoning from my life that reason. Got rid of the reason for the problem: got rid of the problem.

I once worked in the field of special education and one indelible lesson I got from it was: no one is smarter than anyone else. Some of us just require a different tactic or a different way to learn the same things.

EFFORT + QUESTIONS = SUCCESS

At the end of my junior year at Kansas State, I received a dismissal notice for failing to meet academic requirements needed to keep my athletic scholarship. The reality hit me hard. Why couldn't I see the funnel cloud forming before the tornado hit me? It was because my priorities were screwed-up. I had placed more emphasis on partying at the clubs than I had on studying. School work – learning - should have been my first priority, but as an athlete, hanging out with other athletes and the college girls who like to hang with athletes, it was just too easy to get priorities misplaced. I had a choice: study hard, regain my eligibility, or leave school for ... what? I had nothing else. So that summer, I made sure that my academic work was my focus: I went to classes, I did the studying needed, I took notes, I studied late at night and during the weekends – whatever it took, I did not want to look back later and say "I should've done more."

I worked at it and managed to regain my academic standing, which made me once again eligible to participate in athletics.

To be honest, I sweated that one out. I was worried; for the first time, I came fact – to - face with consequences. And I'm proud to say that, maybe for the first time, when the chips were down, I responded in a positive way. I buckled down and cut out the things that were holding me back from succeeding in both the classroom and on the field of athletics. I had forgotten that I was a student first and an athlete second. Once I had that priority straight, I was able to handle other difficulties which came along.

When I experienced a twisted ankle or became frustrated with other players or the coaches, or when the thought crept in that I wasn't getting the attention I had foreseen when I signed the letter of intent, I was able to push all that back and remember that it was the education that came first.

Many potentially great students and athlete have given up on their hopes and dreams. Many have quit school and lived a life of *"If I could of, I would of and I should of."* My academic counselors, Professor Henry Camp and Berry Surtec Sr., advised me during my fall, and gave me an insight to the true value of my priorities and how they relate to my life. They showed me a way out of the darkness when I couldn't see any open windows. I listened to them intently, and their honesty and concern allowed me to open-up, pay attention and take action. I followed their advice step by step. I learned then that talking honestly with counselors was a huge gift that schools provide. Talking openly with them gave me a new and clear vision of who I was and steps I should take to be successful. Yes, I later fell into all of the holes I have written about here, but these two men helped me succeed at Kansas State when I was well on the road to becoming just another lost black athlete discarded on the side of the highway.

Still today, I keep in mind the new and clear visions they shared with me. By the time the summer ended, I had made it! It was the first time in my life that I had earned A's and B's. Everything I had ever gotten or learned was because I kept an open mind for suggestions and advice.

Then my Academic Counselors allowed others to guide me through this journey. The new change created a new fire inside of me. I was filled with confidence. Everything I did or tried from that day forward was achieved without fear.

Efforts and questions were the key to my understanding and comprehension. My athletic career really took off with this new fire: the realization that I could do anything I put my mind to.

I quickly excelled in competitions against several former Olympians and medalists. I adopted a better warm-up stretching routine from watching four-time Olympic gold medalist Carl Lewis.

I learned to train every day and not take a day off from my trainer Steve Miller, because that's what Edwin Moses did. I roomed with Olympic medalist Al Joyner. I ran a photo finish at the 1984 Drake Relays in Iowa and witnessed the famous 100-meter race of Carl Lewis and the NFL's best running-back, Herschel Walker of the Dallas Cowboys. (Herschel Walker was a senior from the University of Georgia who was 6'2" and weighed about 240 lbs. Herschel had lighting speed and he ran neck-and-neck with Carl, only to be edged out by Lewis at the tape.) A teammate of mine, Doug Lytle, made the USA Olympic team in the Pole-Vault event in 1984 and placed sixth.

On August 16th, 2009, a Jamaican Olympian sprinter named Usain Bolt, ran a 9.58 world record run in the 100 meters. He trained hard, but most of all, he believed in himself. Mr. Usain Bolt also broke the world record in the 200-meter dash with 19.19 seconds in August, 2009 at the famous Berlin Olympic Stadium in Germany.

Hard work, coupled with extreme confidence, and knowing his priorities, (plus a large gift of talent) enabled Bolt to this double success.

In 2001, I had the exciting pleasure of running into Channel 7 ABC Sports Reporter, Jim Rose, while shopping at a grocery store in Matteson, Illinois. I talked to him briefly about my long friendship with Craig Hodges (Chicago Bulls legendary basketball player), which led to our discussing the idea of helping youth, especially those suffering from depression.

Mr. Rose surprised me. He's a real down to earth person who cares about others, and this discussion stayed with me through all the dark years.

One morning while incarcerated, I was in the middle of writing a song for my "Contagious Visions" when the Oprah Winfrey Show came on with a special guest, Halle Berry, who spoke of her weakness – "being attracted to love."

As I listened to her insight gained from a broken relationship, she said to Oprah, "I remember that you told me long ago that without integrity, there's no Love." I immediately thought of my family, especially my father and mother, and how close their relationship was. I realized that that is how all the best relationships I knew, including the rest of my family and many friends', grew to be so special and so strong.

My thoughts about relationships were forever changed.

STAYING FOCUSED

I come from a family of good athletes. All of my brothers excelled in track. As a teenager, I grew up with a great group of friends who were also excellent athletes. Many have gone on to become professional athletes as well as teachers and coaches at high schools. We all excelled because of our ability to remain focused, even through tough times. Staying focused is critical for anyone doing just about anything from the largest to the simplest task.

A high school teammate and friend, Craig Hodges, former NBA Champion, would never leave a Chicago Bulls practice until he had made 150 three pointers. This habit brought forth an automatic response to hit his target with great accuracy. If there ever was a person that had an exceptional work ethic in the basketball arena, it was Craig Hodges. He still is tenth all-time in single-season NBA 3-point percentage (4914% in 1987-1988).

I watched, played and practiced with Craig for many years before he became an NBA star. His discipline and determination was second to none. I recall a conversation he had with my dad once when we were all watching the Pirates play the Cubs (yeah, I am one of those die-hard Cub fans, but my dad cheered for any team that played against the Cubs. My father was a Chicago White Sox fan, so you know we used to go at it).

Craig became a vocal and well-known activist, drawing attention to the plight of the poor communities in the United States. In one well-publicized incident, the championship Bulls were invited to meet President H.W. Bush, despite suggestions that he downplay his political beliefs, Craig gave a letter to the President expressing his positions on the government's insufficient concern for the plight of the poor, and especially the African-American poor.

After that day, Craig never saw the NBA again. Sources around the league allegedly spread the word that Craig was a troublemaker. He was one of the greatest pure long-distance shooters in the history of the NBA; his records included:

- most three-point field goals made in a half (5);
- the most three-point field goals made in a quarter (5);
- the most consecutive three point goals made (9);
- the highest free throw percentage (as of 2010) (.900);
- the winner of three consecutive All Star game long distance shootouts.

Craig has since been actively raising money for underprivileged inner-city schools. The point is that he had a goal, and set his mind to "determination" and put in the work and focus to obtain his goal.

But he also set a second goal: working to alleviate conditions for poor children, and he has been tireless in his pursuit of helping those who need it.

Craig's example helped light this new fire to live and change the direction of my life. I know this requires me to focus every day to avoid skidding back to a point of no return. There are going to still be some ups and downs, good times and bad, fast and slow. However, I absolutely believe that if I set solid goals, work tirelessly toward those goals with solid focus then the progress I have experienced so far will continue.

I am fortunate to have a loving, supportive family, and one of the benefits to my new life is no longer have to be ashamed of who I was, or reluctant to face them after another arrest for burglary or theft or any other stupid thing. I can finally be proud of who I am.

AND FINALLY ... (or maybe not so finally!)

In 2004 at the age of forty-four, I had knee surgery to repair bone tissue damaged 20 years earlier, 1984. This knee injury, which ended my track career, was originally from a childhood deformity, but had escalated several weeks prior to the 1984 Olympic trials.

I was sitting in a good position, climbing up the ladder of the ranks of American hurdlers to a number 6 ranking. I was picked as an outside shot to make the Olympic team according to all of the track and field polls. However, they were unaware of my injury. I kept it a secret and no matter how much I tried to focus on the race, all I could think about was the pain. When I failed to advance, my focus and goals dissipated.

Years later, following the knee surgery, the doctors informed me that had I rehabilitated the knee correctly, I would have been able to run and jump not only as fast and as high as before, but even higher than ever.

I lifted weights to strengthen my upper body and legs, then, at age 47, after many years not having played, I picked up a basketball and exploded off the ground to a resounding dunk. I'm once again enjoying basketball and today I play with people in their 20s and 30s.

To believe in hope is the most powerful force in humanity. Anthony Robbins showed me a unique and quick way to move forward from the negative obstacles that had hindered my well-being. In fact, I remember verbatim just about everything that I studied under him, and now I am fortunate to deliver my message in a more practical way.

I recommend that anyone that may be struggling with negative, dark emotions, finances, relationships, substance abuse or homelessness, to look for a good recommended self-help book of motivation (your librarians can recommend the best ones). I learned to adopt beliefs that work for other people.

There's always a way to do better in every aspect of my life, as long as I don't quit trying. My entire life changed from park benches to Park Avenue, from jail to feeling swell. Faith will ignite the fire.

For the future, this new Fire will drive you to a new happiness, and things that you put off will be back on your menu. Things you forgot will come back to you. You will see a new vision and have a much better focus. You will gain a new confidence. This new fire begins when you say, "I'm no longer going to live this way; I deserve better and I will do better."

This NEW FIRE began when I was able to tell myself, "I'm not going to quit." This new fire is called Desire. The new fire begins when I said, "I'm not taking it anymore, and from now on I'm going to start treating myself better."

When we say these things to ourselves, we automatically raise our standards to a higher level; I know that our self-esteem will amazingly begin to change because I have experienced it!

This new Fire! Begins today.

Depression had brought me to an all-time low; it had me fill out applications to get permanent disability. I thought that when I turned 40, I wouldn't be able to play basketball as well as I could in my younger years, and now at 47-48 years old, I am still dunking the ball. It is all because I set a new goal and commitment to practice, jogging, and strengthening the areas that would increase my ability. I began to do explosive training movements.

The Power in us is much greater than the power that tries to hold us back. I had to focus on what's right and not what's wrong. I had to keep setting goals and focusing on these goals. A voice in my head urged me: "Don't put it off any longer, start making changes now!"

My former track coaches at Kansas State in the mid-80s, John Capriotti, Gregg Kraft, McVey and Randy Cole, have all been successful and are presently enjoying the fruits of their labored success.

They were a part of my village and circumference that helped shape my confidence and character as a student-athlete. They also have a great sense of humor.

One particular day, the head coach, Steve Miller, suggested that we could work on my weakness or we can build on my strengths, with reference to training in my senior year in track and making a run to qualify for the Olympic Team. We decided to focus on my strengths. He then put me with the middle-distance runners for a two-month training period. We ran repeat 800s, 8-10 of them over hilly gravel surfaces, while Randy Cole helped increase my mileage run from 2.5 to 6 miles. I would have never, ever believed that I could have jogged 6 miles, but the coaches were skilled at discerning the best approach for each athlete, teaching the athletes the methods they designed, explaining the benefits, and then mapping out the specific steps, objectives, and ultimate goal.

They never put the emphasis on winning. Instead, the emphasis was on competing and the possibilities would take care of themselves.

Today, Gregg Kraft, besides being the former Arizona State track coach, was one of the 2008 Division I, Track and Field Champion Coaches, and Coach Capriotti is an excellent coach and influential in the world-wide marketing of Track and Field.

The point I am making is that the success in these men's lives was a strength to me. For example, when Steve Miller and these other great men surrounded themselves with other intelligent, positive, and open-minded people who committed themselves to character - building blocks of success like desire, effort, stick-to-itiveness, good attitude, and the willingness to study and learn, they created a village network of support within Kansas State University, and this "village" attitude rubbed-off on me and I saw it influence other athletes who "bought into" their philosophy.

Anyone who had even an iota of potential, these coaches knew how to maximize it.

Staying focused is what usually separates those who are able to perform in competition at maximum levels, even as the pressure mounts, from those who never make it. It is not just in athletics; in all aspects of life, I have learned the value of setting goals, because goals give me direction. Whenever I have found myself drifting away from my goals due to life's circumstance, which at times have caused changes in my course, I reach back to the simplicity of focusing on my goals, which allows me to then re-connect the dots that always leads me back to what is important.

I have seen many people who had or have projects that have been put on the back burner for years, and they ended up living a life of regret. I am example that we do not have to live a life of regrets; we are able to, and we should, always "GO for It!" and see what the unforeseen in my life has for you.

I am sure many of my poor decisions angered Coach Miller and filled him with disappointment. However, He never judged me. He drew out the potential in me by still believing in me. His belief helped me to believe stronger and focus on using my time, talent and gifts to help others. This was the tipping point for me, and I have been focused and on fire to leave a legacy of "helping others" ever since. I wrote this book 3 ½ years, before it was printed, thanks to a conversation with my former coach, Steve Miller, which re-lit the fire in my life to get beyond the past wreckage of my life. Because I was willing to reach out to others, I realized I do not need to remain a victim, and can go on to once again succeed in my endeavors. I know how difficult the teenage years can be. No longer a child, but not yet an adult.

Our bodies change physically and it often seems like we don't fit in or belong anywhere, but I now know that every person --- every person --- is precious and can go on to accomplish great things, despite the many obstacles that may be in our paths.

We are blessed to live in a country, even with all of its faults, that has tremendous resources of every kind to help us overcome and be a success. It is important for us all to recognize the importance of education; it is the key to breaking out of the cycle of poverty, confusion and depression in which many of us find ourselves caught.

Thanks for reading. It means a lot to me, and I hope my story can inspire you to "Go for it!"

QUESTIONS FOR FURTHER THOUGHTS AND DISCUSSION

1. What are the most important values in my life? Make a list, putting the most important at the top. Then, under each one, list the steps you are taking to reveal these values in your acts and attitudes. Next to this list, list what you are doing which undermine or hide these values.

2. What is about myself that I wish other people to know? For example, do I like to read? Draw? Play baseball or another sport? WHY do I wish other people knew this about me?

3. What is it I wish I could start or finish THIS MONTH. What is it that is preventing me from achieving this accomplishment? List the steps, on a timeline, that I will take to start, progress, and complete.

4.   What is it that I procrastinate doing? It could be fixing something on your car, or studying, or writing a play, or homework. Why do I procrastinate? List the benefits and liabilities of procrastinating, then make a promise to yourself that you will make an effort to finish what is needed as early as possible (this allows more time to do more things you *want* to do).

5.   What negative habits do I have that impedes my success in any particular area?

6.   Which of my relationships are contributing positively to my life, and which are having a negative influence. Make a list of the reasons for each and steps you can take to emphasize the positive relationships and reduce the influence of the others.

7.   Who can I trust to discuss my deepest feelings, my hardest problems? If there is no one, research counselors available to you. You might or might not proceed to visit one, but the search will give you a list of resources you may someday want to use.

8.   How can I reduce the stress in my life? Sometimes friends unknowingly add stress in our lives by demanding all our time, or pressuring us to go where or do something we know is not good for us.

9.   What do I want to achieve in 6 months? 12 months? Write a list and, under each one, write what you are doing to achieve each. Post this list on your wall where you will see it every day.

10. What am I afraid of? Why? Is my fear a warning to avoid this, or is it telling me I am mis-interpreting a situation? Think this through carefully and fully.

11. Meditate at least 10 minutes each day. Think of the colors and sounds you like, things you like to do, who you really are.

For guest appearances or book orders, please send email to...

juliusmercer6doc@gmail.com

and/or call

1-773-793-8669.

Made in the USA
Middletown, DE
09 May 2021

39312098R00106